Kathey K.

Implementing Supplier Diversity

Driver of Entrepreneurship

palgrave
macmillan

Kathey K. Porter
BusinessFAB Media
Gainesville, FL, USA

ISBN 978-3-319-94393-0   ISBN 978-3-319-94394-7   (eBook)
https://doi.org/10.1007/978-3-319-94394-7

© The Editor(s) (if applicable) and The Author(s) 2019

This work is subject to copyright. All rights are solely and exclusively licensed by the Publisher, whether the whole or part of the material is concerned, specifically the rights of translation, reprinting, reuse of illustrations, recitation, broadcasting, reproduction on microfilms or in any other physical way, and transmission or information storage and retrieval, electronic adaptation, computer software, or by similar or dissimilar methodology now known or hereafter developed.

The use of general descriptive names, registered names, trademarks, service marks, etc. in this publication does not imply, even in the absence of a specific statement, that such names are exempt from the relevant protective laws and regulations and therefore free for general use.

The publisher, the authors and the editors are safe to assume that the advice and information in this book are believed to be true and accurate at the date of publication. Neither the publisher nor the authors or the editors give a warranty, express or implied, with respect to the material contained herein or for any errors or omissions that may have been made. The publisher remains neutral with regard to jurisdictional claims in published maps and institutional affiliations.

Cover image © Artur Debat / Moment / Getty

This Palgrave Macmillan imprint is published by the registered company Springer Nature Switzerland AG.
The registered company address is: Gewerbestrasse 11, 6330 Cham, Switzerland

Implementing Supplier Diversity

Foreword

Friday, April 5, 1968, started out like any other school day for me. I took the bus from my Shepherd Park neighborhood in Washington, DC, down Georgia Avenue to Missouri Avenue, where I got off to go to school at Paul Jr. High School. Not long after arriving, however, I realized that this day was like no other. The Reverend Dr. Martin Luther King Jr. had been assassinated the night before in Memphis, Tennessee. By morning, African Americans were in the streets expressing their rage and hopelessness in more than 100 cities across the country. Around 10 a.m., our principal got on the school's public address system; informed the teachers, staff and students that school was dismissed; and told us that we should try our best to get home safely. By the time we were dismissed, smoke and fires were visible from Georgia Avenue, one of the main arteries running through the heart of the city, from Shepherd Park past Howard University to the National Mall near the White House. The buses had stopped running throughout the city and in their place were military transport vehicles loaded with fully armed National Guardsmen, ready for war.

Before this paroxysm of urban revolt, Dr. King had begun to pivot from talking about civil rights and voting rights for African Americans to speaking about economic rights. Dr. King was in Memphis to support striking African American garbage workers when he gave his final address, in which he said the following:

> We don't have to argue with anybody. We don't have to curse and go around acting bad with our words. We don't need any bricks and bottles. We don't need any Molotov cocktails. We just need to go around to these stores, and to these massive industries in our country and say, "God sent us here, to say to you that you're not

treating his children right. And we've come by here to ask you to make the first item on your agenda fair treatment, where God's children are concerned. Now, if you are not prepared to do that, we do have an agenda that we must follow. And our agenda calls for withdrawing economic support from you."

And so, as a result of this we are asking you tonight, to go out and tell your neighbors not to buy Coca-Cola in Memphis. Go by and tell them not to buy Sealtest milk. As Jesse Jackson has said, up to now, only the garbage men have been feeling pain; now we must kind of redistribute the pain.

African Americans, leaders in corporate America, and the White House all heard these words loud and clear. Later that same year, George Johnson, the president and CEO of Western Electric (now AT&T), came together with several organizations, including the Chicago Economic Development Organization, the Chicago Urban League and the Cosmopolitan Chamber of Commerce, to hold the first Chicago Business Opportunity Fair. After that event, the Chicago Minority Purchasing Council was formed. Robert M. Stuart, the president and CEO of National Can, became the first chairperson of the nascent organization, which eventually became the National Minority Supplier Development Council (NMSDC). Johnson was instrumental in recruiting other corporate leaders from across the country and garnering the support of the US Department of Commerce. From these humble beginnings, the NMSDC was formed in 1972.

Eight months after the assassination of Dr. King, Richard Nixon became president. President Nixon was elected largely as the white reaction to the turbulent urban unrest and the anti-war student movement. His "silent majority" rhetoric was an attempt to return America to a more comfortable time. But in his conservatism, Nixon saw an opportunity to connect with African Americans by appealing to "Black capitalism," which was ideologically consistent with his conservative economic principles. Black capitalism also served as a counter to the growing Black Power movement that he and other conservative leaders saw as an existential threat to America. Black capitalism was a way for the black community to reconnect to the Republican Party and to the mainstream economy. In Nixon's view, black capitalism could be the basis for a private-sector-driven, anti-poverty program.

Supplier diversity is impossible to understand fully without an appreciation for the political dynamics that drove American society in the late 1960s and early 1970s. And with those changes and later developments, the reasons for opening the US economy to minority businesses also changed. While the delineation of distinct periods is not an exact science, there are at least three discrete periods that have provided rationales for supplier diversity. These periods include the following:

- Compliance with Federal Law
- The Right Thing to Do
- The Business Case for Supplier Diversity

It is important to note that these periods do not coincide for all corporations or all public sector organizations. Some companies are ahead of others, and some are behind. Further, none of these periods are inherently superior to the others in terms of their impact on minority business development. It is possible that any one of these periods could result in significant improvements in diverse business development, at least for short periods.

Compliance with federal law was a powerful force that contributed to the development of hundreds of successful minority businesses, which won contracts because federal agencies and their prime contractors were under regulatory pressure to provide those contracts to minority firms. Legal challenges to compliance ended this regime of supplier diversity and led to a corporation-dominated effort based on corporate social responsibility. Supplier diversity was a way for corporations to demonstrate their commitment to the larger community of stakeholders, including minority businesses. But as a new cohort of corporate leaders came to power, all of whom were a generation removed from the civil rights struggle of the 1960s, there was a reversion to basic business principles. Books like *Good to Great* and *In Search of Excellence* reinvigorated corporate America's focus on long-term profitability and a dedication to corporate metrics and performance. Supplier diversity had to support its claim on scarce corporate resources like all internal corporate departments. Supplier diversity leaders were now in a different phase, one in which they began to make the business case for supplier diversity. An effective business case had to demonstrate that the use of diverse businesses contributed to corporate profitability. This bottom-line focus was supported with hard data, something the advocates for the "feel good" approach simply could not do.

Significant social, economic and technological forces were important determinants in the evolution of supplier diversity from the "compliance" era to the "right thing to do" era to the "business case" era. Forces like globalization, supply chain optimization, strategic procurement, industry consolidation, domestic income distribution and national and local political forces impact the ways that corporations manage all of their supply chain, including diverse suppliers. It is likely that these forces will continue to influence supplier diversity in the future.

Compliance with Federal Law (1969–1990)

On March 5, 1969, less than three weeks into his administration, President Nixon issued Executive Order 11458. The order created the Office of Minority Business Enterprise, which later became the Minority Business Development Agency within the Department of Commerce. The order also served as the basis for the Small Business Administration's 8(a) Business Development Program for minority sole-source contracts (set-asides). In October 1971, Nixon issued Executive Order 11625, which allowed for public support of private organizations like the NMSDC in order to promote the development of minority businesses. According to section 1(a)(4) of the order:

> The Secretary of Commerce (hereinafter referred to as "the Secretary") shall … within constraints of law and appropriations therefore, and according to his discretion, provide financial assistance to public and private organizations so that they may render technical and management assistance to minority business enterprises, and defray all or part of the costs of pilot or demonstration projects conducted by public or private agencies or organizations which are designed to overcome the special problems of minority business enterprises or otherwise to further the purposes of this order.

These two executive orders and Public Law 95-507 (1978) ushered in an era of minority business development in federal government contracting based on a regime of compliance. The Department of Defense, the largest federal department, used its considerable buying power and these executive orders to force large defense contractors to contract with eligible minority businesses. Departments and agencies within the federal government established the Office of Small and Disadvantaged Business Utilization (OSDBU) to track their organizations' spend as well as the spend of large prime contractors with eligible minority businesses.

The effectiveness of compliance for minority businesses becomes obvious when reviewing the top black businesses of the period. In 1980, *Black Enterprise* magazine published a list of the largest African American enterprises. The list was dominated by automobile retail dealers, retail oil distributors, cosmetics companies, publishers and food service companies. Of the top 100 companies, only 13 were or could have been major suppliers to corporations or to the federal government. While this could certainly be considered progress, it demonstrated that ten years after Executive Order 11458 and one year after Public Law 95-507, the largest African American–owned firms were still concentrated on supplying goods and services to African American consumers rather than to large corporations. Breaking into corporate supply chains was still a major challenge during the compliance era. By 2017, however, the five largest firms on the *Black Enterprise* list of the largest African American companies were suppliers to corporations, and seven of the ten largest companies were suppliers.

The early years of minority business development were dominated by these public interventions in markets, but it was not long before there was a backlash against laws and executive orders designed to promote minority business development. In *City of Richmond v. Croson* (1989), the Supreme Court ruled that the City of Richmond's 10% set-aside law for local minority businesses was unconstitutional. In *Adarand Constructors, Inc. v. Pena* (1995), the Supreme Court ruled that federal set-aside laws based on race were an unconstitutional violation of the Fourteenth Amendment. The combination of these two Supreme Court rulings all but ended public sector leadership in minority business development and brought an effective close to the age of compliance.

The Right Thing to Do (1990s–early 2000s)

In 1988, Harriet Michel became president and CEO of the National Minority Supplier Development Council (NMSDC), and she saw the writing on the wall. Michel transformed NMSDC from a publicly funded organization to an organization funded by large corporations. Under Michel's leadership, the number of regional affiliates grew, the number of corporate members increased to 3500 and the number of certified minority businesses increased to 16,000.

In addition to the organizational growth, there was also a transformation in the motivation for supplier diversity, which ushered in the next phase of supplier diversity, one not based on compliance. During this era, corporations began hiring supplier diversity professionals who were responsible for being the "gate-keepers" for minority businesses attempting to access corporate opportunities. Their role internally was to search out opportunities for the growing number of certified minority businesses. These supplier diversity leaders engaged in these activities because these corporations' customer bases and workforces were becoming increasingly diverse and because they believed that minority businesses should have access to corporate opportunities. Corporations routinely referenced and discussed their supplier diversity efforts in their annual reports, often noting that it was the "right thing to do."

Understanding the need to validate their existence within organizations and to advocate harder for the minority businesses that they represented, supplier diversity professionals in this era also began documenting their utilization and spending with diverse suppliers. Corporations invested in portals to collect information on diverse suppliers seeking to do business with their companies. Diverse businesses grew frustrated with these portals because they were viewed as "black holes," where data went in but no opportunities came out. In the early days of vendor management systems, analytics and dashboards could be extremely clumsy and cumbersome, but this was obviously not the case for all suppliers and all companies. Thousands of companies received their opportunities through these systems, which large corporations used to keep track of everything. Minority business utilization needed to conform to these systems, even if it reduced the impact of the relationship approach for securing corporate business.

During this phase, supplier diversity professionals were prized for their relationship building skills and their ability to support the growing demands of certified diverse businesses. Relationships between certified minority business owners and supplier diversity professionals were key to the success of a diverse business. These supplier diversity professionals used moral suasion to change buying patterns within corporate America. This approach obviously has its limits, one of which is the willingness of corporate buyers to compromise on "non-essential" products and services but not on the goods and services that are mission critical. It is easy to understand why diverse businesses found success in crowded industries like corporate gifts, travel, cleaning services and supplies, limousine services and other low-barrier-to-entry industries during this era. While contracting organizations enjoyed competitive pricing on these goods and services, diverse business owners found that they were playing in an increasingly overcrowded industry that offered little margins and few opportunities to really scale the business.

Thus, diverse business began to shift their attention to those areas that represented the "real money"—these areas that were critical functions within the corporate supply chain offered substantially larger contracts and represented high growth and scalability for their companies, such as construction, manufacturing or IT. This was where the big boys were playing and diverse business wanted in.

The Business Case for Supplier Diversity (2000s–Present)

Supplier diversity professionals occupy a middle ground between diverse businesses attempting to supply goods and services to their companies and the buyers and other corporate stakeholders who look to them to provide information on diverse suppliers for buying opportunities. Supplier diversity professionals are advocates for diverse businesses, but they are primarily subject to the strategic direction of their employers.

This era has also been supported by the arrival of two new diversity organizations that built on the success of the NMSDC. In 1997, the Women's Business Enterprise National Council (WBENC) was formed to assist the growing needs of non-minority women entrepreneurs seeking access to corporate business. In 2001, the Billion Dollar Roundtable (BDR) was created to celebrate the extraordinary accomplishments of large corporations, each of which had achieved at least $1 billion in first-tier procurement with certified diverse businesses. In 2017, the Billion Dollar Roundtable reported 27 member organizations with more than $77 billion in combined spend with certified diverse businesses. The BDR and the WBENC brought fresh insights, new methods and increased visibility to the overall mission of increasing diversity in corporate supply chains, based not on feelings or "right thing to do" notions but on unapologetic business interests.

The interests that initiated the business case for supplier diversity had three legs. One was the changing demographics of consumers, both domestically and internationally. The second was the internal feedback that supported supplier diversity when large companies "demanded" supplier diversity performance information from the other large companies they sought to do business with. The third was the realization that no one ethnic group or gender had a monopoly on solving corporate problems, which led companies to adopt supplier diversity strategies as a way to harness innovation and technology. There are several top corporate supplier diversity programs that espouse this philosophy, but in my opinion, few say it better than Toyota:

> Toyota is committed to having a supplier base which more closely reflects our customers and the diversity of our team members who build Toyota vehicles in North America. Having a diverse supplier base enables us to contribute to the economic well-being of all segments of the North American population. Also we recognize that partnering with suppliers who provide a diversity of ideas—in addition to delivering manufacturing support, goods, and services—creates a significant competitive advantage for Toyota.

If corporate leaders are not convinced that demographics and innovation are powerful forces for the sustainability of a company and an industry, they should look to the consumer behavior impacting most industries due to changing demographics. Younger consumers are having a profound effect on the auto industry because they are asking heretical questions like this: Do I really need to own a car? The travel industry is affected by, again, younger consumers asking: Do I really need to stay in a traditional hotel? The food industry is impacted by consumers asking: Do I really need to go to a grocery store or a restaurant? Behind each of these questions is a disruptive technology that is upending traditional business models. Further, companies that are not in tune with the growing diversity in consumer markets may find themselves in indefensible situations and negatively impacted with customers questioning whether the company's values and priorities are in line with their own. And let us not forget, this sentiment also extends from the culture of the organization and the employees that it hires, all the way up to the boardroom and the directors that it appoints to its board. If diversity is to truly permeate through all aspects of the organization, there is no reason why these directives cannot be driven by innovative, diverse companies led by women, ethnic and racial minorities.

Supplier diversity has blossomed over the last two decades to create a bio-system that has spurred further expansion. As more corporations adopt supplier diversity programs, more corporate leaders are asking their large, non-minority corporate suppliers questions about their own supplier diversity efforts. Today, supplier diversity professionals spend a significant amount of time responding to requests from internal sales colleagues for help with bids to acquire new business from large corporations. For example, if General Motors seeks business with Avis, Avis might ask about the status of GM's supplier diversity program. This has the effect of driving more spend with diverse suppliers and improving supplier diversity programs throughout corporate America.

The strong business case for supplier diversity is sustainable in ways that the compliance and "right thing to do" models are not. We have seen how laws that were written to promote supplier diversity within government can be shredded with a single Supreme Court ruling. We have also seen that appeals to emotion and conscience often fall on deaf ears in a corporate milieu driven by metrics. Ultimately, good feelings are the consequence of successful business outcomes and actions, not the cause of those actions.

I would be remiss if I did not include my thoughts on what the future holds for supplier diversity. The distinct periods identified earlier are all built on the successes and failures of the preceding periods. The next disruption of supplier diversity will be no different, but because this is far from an exact science, only time will tell what the next phase of the supplier diversity movement will look like. I suspect that we will see a return to the original intent of supplier diversity, which was to improve the economic conditions of communities. We do not need or want a return to the 1960s, when cities regularly burned, but we know that minority business development is perhaps the most powerful force in integrating communities and spreading and creating wealth. I hope that corporations will continue to lead in this effort and that the diverse business owners will continue to see their success tied to the success of the broader community. I have had the privilege to be part of all of the phases discussed earlier, and I am excited to see the next supplier diversity disruption.

It is my great pleasure to contribute to this compendium on supplier diversity that Kathey has assembled. Enjoy!

School of Business   Fred McKinney
Quinnipiac University
Hamden, CT, USA

Preface: Why Supplier Diversity?

Supplier diversity is a business strategy that ensures a diverse supplier base in the procurement of goods and services for any business or organization. It emphasizes the creation of a diverse supply chain that works to secure the inclusion of diverse groups in the procurement plans for government, not-for-profits, and private industry. Supplier diversity, as we know it today, is one of the least researched and written about strategic business development topics. But in today's increasingly competitive global marketplace, supplier diversity is a strategy that cannot be overlooked by either global organizations or small businesses.

The concept of supplier diversity began via executive order nearly 50 years ago; however, organizational purchasing activities have been around for thousands of years. Before we get into the heart of the book, it is central to understand the purchasing function and its evolution.

A (Brief) History—From Purchasing to Procurement: Purchasing is an old profession, yet it is thought of similarly to insurance; you don't think about it until you need it. Despite procurement-related tasks being noted and dating back as early as 3000 BC in Egypt, it has attracted little attention from historians. In Egypt, scribes responsible for pyramid design also functioned as clerks, using papyrus to record the amount of labor and materials needed for construction. Ancient Romans also used scribes to create contracts when the empire was engaged in trade with private suppliers.

In the late 1890s, toward the end of the Industrial Revolution, corporations started incorporating the purchasing functions in their operations; however, it was still largely considered clerical work. During World Wars I and II, the purchasing function increased due to the need to get materials to produce supplies for the war and keep the factories and mines operating during this time. It was during the 1950s and 1960s that purchasing really began to gain visibility within organizations as performance techniques became more refined and as the number of trained professionals increased but still purchasing agents were basically order-placing clerical personnel serving in a staff-support position.

In the late 1960s and early 1970s, purchasing personnel aligned their focus on materials management. As strategic planning became more important for organizations, materials management became an integral part of that strategy, along with lean production techniques from Japan, thus increasing the relevancy of the purchasing department. By the 1970s, the oil embargo and the shortage of many basic raw materials brought much of the business world's focus to the purchasing arena. During the 1980s, the advent of just-in-time purchasing techniques and the emphasis on inventory control and supplier quality, quantity, timing, and dependability made purchasing a cornerstone of competitive strategy.

The 1990s brought a focus on value proposition and strategic sourcing. Organizations began to realize they could negotiate better pricing and terms, thus placing an increased focus on cost savings and ROI. During the 2000s, organizations also began incorporating enterprise resources planning or ERP systems, which allowed them to continuously monitor, re-evaluate, and improve the overall purchasing activities of an organization. They also began incorporating long-term contracts to facilitate better pricing for longer periods of time. However, in order for this strategy to work, organizations knew that they would need strong supplier data as well as buy in from the suppliers. This gave rise to the need to shift the focus from strictly price to supplier relationship building and supplier management. Further, as organizations have increased their reliance on technology, suppliers have emerged as key business partners in driving new technological breakthroughs to drive down costs as technology also continues to rapidly evolve, redefining the way organizations procure and source, locally, nationally, and globally.

For a long time, the purchasing function was solely focused on price—getting the desired goods and service at the lowest, reasonable price. We now know that with this strategy, you often get what you pay for. Arguably, it was during this time that the adoption of a stronger focus on supplier relationship building and the increased importance on this function, that many organizations began changing their name from purchasing to procurement. In doing research for this book, many procurement agents indicated that the name change reflected a thoughtful industry shift in the perception of the role itself, its place within the organization, and future-forward thinking, thus transitioning from solely a purchasing *function* of ordering, receiving, and paying for goods or services to a more holistic view of the overall procurement *process* which is a larger, more encompassing organizational function for establishing fundamental requirements, performing market research, evaluating and selecting vendors, and negotiating contracts.

After nearly a century in the shadows, procurement has finally become a major function with immense importance to an organization's bottom line and the value that it brings. It continues to advance with a more holistic focus on the complete supply chain.

What Is a Supply Chain, Anyway?

Globalization has transformed the way the world does business, especially for international commercial transactions where there is a significant focus on outsourcing key resources (such as labor) to maximize economic growth. To ensure the success of these transactions, the relevant "chain of suppliers" have had to consistently deliver quality goods and services to the marketplace, while simultaneously remaining competitive to stay in business. Of course, this is no easy feat for any supplier. The good news, however, is that the process is equal parts art and science.

A supply chain is the ecosystem of suppliers needed to create a single product for a company. The "chain" is comprised of several "links" that include everything from raw materials to services that are all—in one way or another—components of the finished product. There is an order and function for each link, which explains why they are connected so purposefully. There are also economic and opportunity costs associated with each link, which is why selecting the most appropriate suppliers is critical to product development, marketing, and sales.

Supply chain management (SCM) takes the concept of the "chain" a few steps further. It describes the flow of goods, services, and related activities executed from inception to consumption required to plan, control, and achieve a product's overall success. There are six key components that structure the process: planning, sourcing, making, delivering, returning, and enabling. In most cases, these components are streamlined to achieve the most scalable and cost-effective distribution possible. Here's what a snippet of what supply chain management looks like in practice: It begins with a focus on a company's production materials (the "inputs"), which each incur a cost recovered in the final price of the finished product. Take widgets for example. It's here that the idea of market competition comes into play, escalating the notion that prices should be kept low without sacrificing the quality of the goods provided. Think using the most cost-effective materials to construct the widgets without sacrificing their quality. By closely monitoring costs from all sources and keeping a close eye on operational procedures, supply chain management works to effectively maximize value and resources through increased efficiency and profitability.

Some companies such as Coca-Cola® view sustainability as a core value of supply chain management. This perspective allows them to make an impact beyond their own operations to improve the environment, livelihoods, and society. Leveraging the concept of farm-to-table agriculture, especially with products such as sugarcane, has helped them to successfully achieve this goal. TOMS® shoes and accessories is another great example of sustainable supply chain management. Its products are all made from environmentally friendly materials, and it donates proceeds from every product sold to help someone in need through its One for One® campaign.

While supply chain management is not necessarily a simple process, there are clear benefits for those who do it well. End users get high-quality products at good prices. They accomplish long-term, overarching business goals through the efficiencies gained through selective outsourcing. Successful suppliers in this otherwise "labyrinthine business chain" achieve economic growth, repeat customers, and expanded sourcing opportunities, even while navigating competition, increased risk, and complex management issues. The goal, then, for every link in the chain is to become proficient in the (SCM) process and maximize their overall success.

When I began working in supplier diversity over ten years ago, there were not many published resources that I could readily access to get information on growing and running an effective supplier diversity program. While there were national organizations and professionals within them, organizational budgets did not always allow for you to attend a national conference for four or five days to get information, nor did I have the network that I have today where I could call a colleague with a question or two (or three). Early on, much of what I did was based on my instincts as an entrepreneur, by talking to other business owners about what they needed and, occasionally, following the Nike motto, "Just Do It." While it has gotten much easier to find information because there is an extensive network of professionals to call upon and there are numerous events and resource groups with whom one can stay engaged, it still remains a woefully underwritten topic considering its relevancy in entrepreneurial development. I am proud to say that I am now part of that resource community and frequently get calls, emails, and even visits from colleagues to talk about the industry and offer any assistance.

I have had the fortunate opportunity to assist many small and diverse businesses grow and scale up with help from supplier diversity programs. I am a firm believer that if possible, every business should have a business-to-business strategy for selling goods and services to an institutional customer. I have seen, firsthand, how firms can successfully navigate a sometimes complex and fragmented system to positively impact their businesses by using these programs. Coordinated introductions, networking and meet-and-greet events, matchmaking sessions, mentor/protégé programs, business development conferences and workshops, recommendations on policies and procedures, and collaborations with other entities are just some of the ways that businesses can find the resources, personnel, and information needed to be successful in a highly competitive and ever-changing business environment.

One example is Markesia and Korey Akinbami of Ducere Construction Services of Atlanta, a minority construction trades firm, focusing on residential and light commercial painting projects. I met them at a small business event and we ended up having dinner. Over dinner, we were discussing their business, and I asked if they ever considered focusing more on the commercial side and doing business with institutional customers. They expressed an interest but were tentative as they had never done business with a large institution and were not sure about the process. I assured them if they were willing to start out in a mentor-protégé program which allowed them to partner with a larger, established business in the area and take the time to build the necessary relationships, they would eventually be a success. To my pleasant surprise, their results surpassed even my expectations.

They dutifully came to program meetings, met with contracting officials, and had a definitive plan of action for what they wanted to accomplish with their mentor. Unbeknownst to me, they also attended courses to help them in areas where they knew they did not have the strongest skill sets including estimating and preparing bids. Through their mentor, they were able to start working on small projects in the $10,000–$25,000 range. As they successfully completed projects, they gained a positive reputation around town with other prime, general contracting/construction management firms as a strong subcontractor. Within a year, they had amassed a portfolio of over ten projects. More importantly, they established relationships with the contracting officers which resulted in them winning an annual painting contact and also provided the foundation for them to win contracts as a prime vendor. Their successful past performance gave them the confidence to branch out and starting winning projects in other markets. In less than three years, their persistence, successful past performance, and business acumen made them a highly sought-after minority firm as they have gone on to be part of various teams, presenting on projects valued at

$10 million or more. They were recently a minority partner on a major project valued at nearly $100 million and are studying to get their general contractors' license. Their tremendous achievements also made it an easy decision to have Ducere mentor other minority firms, particularly women-owned businesses to successfully navigate supplier diversity programs and prepare them to do business with institutional customers. Additionally, their successful performance with the University of Florida served as a springboard for landing contracts with other higher education institutions including the University of South Florida.

While Markesia and Korey Akinbami were successful entrepreneurs prior to starting this business, they quickly grasped the concept of leveraging performance into sustainable growth. Undoubtedly, the impact of supplier diversity was almost instantaneous in their business, allowing them to gain critical insights, shorten their learning and incubating curve, and immediately build the business into a scalable and successful enterprise.

Throughout this book, you will hear from many supplier diversity professionals, thought leaders, and entrepreneurs discussing their experiences either creating or leading supplier diversity to utilizing these programs to build their business. However, there is one thing that everyone will attest to—supplier diversity is at a crossroads and faces tremendous challenges. While there are many organizations with programs that are still in their infancy (1–3 years), there are countless companies and agencies with mature programs that have been around for 20 years or more. As noted in the Foreword, as the supplier diversity industry continues to grow, expand, and evolve, identifying the next disruption will mean that organizations will have to do more than just make the business case.

Like most industries, if you asked a group of professionals the challenges that the supplier diversity industry faces today, you would likely get a myriad of responses. Based on my numerous conversations with supplier diversity colleagues, practitioners, experts, and small businesses, I have identified a few challenges that still exist in spite of the longevity of the industry. It is these challenges that provide the framework for this book.

Section I—Creation, Evolution, and Emergence of Supplier Diversity Programs

Remaining Relevant Amid Constant Change. The ever-changing organizational landscape (e.g., shifting priorities, consolidations for efficiency, and globalization) can make it difficult at best for companies to operate an effective and impactful supplier diversity program while also maintaining a level of influence and relevancy for the small business community.

Section II—Driving Entrepreneurship

Continuing to Create Paths That Connect to Opportunity. Increasingly, organizations are seeing small businesses as the backbone of our economic landscape and as the cornerstone of our communities which power the economic engine. In a thriving, inclusive, and diverse economy, small businesses are key drivers of job creation and growth, but it can be difficult for small businesses, particularly diverse businesses, to compete for those growth dollars. Supplier diversity programs can offer the tools necessary to bring together the business connections and resources to facilitate growth opportunities and to impact the fabric of the community. Why? Because a contract is not just a transaction, it is college tuition, an investment in equipment, or hiring a new employee. It is this expansion that allows a community to thrive, grow, and prosper.

Section III—Designing an Effective Supplier Diversity Program

Creating Business-Centered Rather Than Process-Centered Programs. While some risk management and scrutiny are certainly needed to prevent an organization from overstepping the law, supplier diversity programs often operate from a process-centered perspective rather than a business-centered perspective. Many programs are inherently and needlessly burdensome. For example, often times, the administrative paperwork required to prove diversity and comply with program requirements can be perceived as a huge burden and a costly endeavor. Consequently, many potentially high-performing businesses opt to "avoid the headache" and go a different route. Inevitably, this prohibits businesses from considering supplier diversity as a truly viable business strategy.

Section IV—Helping Entrepreneurs Use Supplier Diversity Programs to Scale

Effective Succession Planning for a Continued Business Pipeline. Despite the advantages that supplier diversity programs can offer and regardless of the geographic location, one of the most common complaints that I hear from supplier diversity professionals is that there are an insufficient number of minority businesses to adequately supply their procurement needs. It is no secret that diverse businesses tend to be smaller and lack the financial resources and/or physical infrastructure to compete with large suppliers, which means that organizations will continue to struggle to identify and obtain minority suppliers who can provide adequate scale and service. Moreover, the trend toward the consolidation and streamlining of the supply base creates even higher hurdles for minority suppliers because contracts and organizations will become dependent upon fewer suppliers. While millennials increasingly seek entrepreneurship as a path to economic freedom, few look at business-to-business opportunities and consider institutional customers such as higher education institutions, corporations, hospitals, and governments as a potential customer base to grow and scale their business endeavors. Encouraging and supporting that next generation of diverse suppliers will be key to ensuring that industries have a sufficient number of firms in which to engage.

Section V—The Future of Supplier Diversity Programs

Technology, Changing Demographics, and Making the "New" Business Case. Everyone wants to know what the future holds. This industry is no different. Whether it is the impact of technology, changing demographics, or the ability to succinctly make the case for having or continuing a program (or all three combined), there are few things that will shape what this industry looks like in the next 10, 20, or 50 years.

It is no secret that many large or small organizations have not always invested in technology to manage their supplier diversity spend and program performance analytics. Instead, they opt to rely on a patchwork of antiquated systems that do not provide a true picture of the landscape and outdated policies that neither encourage new businesses to enter the procurement pipeline nor keep them engaged once they enter the system.

As businesses embrace accurate metrics tracking and compliance reporting for their senior leadership and community stakeholders, a new industry has cropped up, one comprised of companies that specialize in very sophisticated tools to address this need, which requires yet another justification for making the investment.

According to the *Supply and Demand Chain Executive*, it is a well-known fact that minorities will become the majority in the coming decades in the United States. Naturally, the changing demographics have also led to an increase in the number and types of small businesses being started by minorities. For example, between 1997 and 2002, the number of women-owned firms overall increased by 19.8%, according to the "Small Business Economy" report to the president last year. Contrary to popular belief that diverse businesses generally provide commoditized products and services, large proportions of those firms are in the professional, scientific, and technical fields. If firms continue to look for and find new and capable suppliers, chances are that many of them will be diverse suppliers.

While the statistics paint a very clear and convincing picture of the changing demographics and the need for organizations to be responsive, I would be remiss if I did not provide the historical context for the purchasing function which led to rise in supplier relationship management and supplier diversity.

Gainesville, FL   Kathey K. Porter

Acknowledgments

Thank you to the incredible team at Palgrave Macmillan and to my editorial team for your belief, continued support, and tremendous insights. You have helped create a book that we can all be proud of and that represents the industry well. Thank you to the many colleagues, contributors, and collaborators who conspired to make this book happen. I appreciate you more than you know. We are on a mission to help small businesses and diverse entrepreneurs and to elevate the industry. I am proud to call you friends. Thank you also to the entrepreneurs and small businesses with whom I work every day. Your successes are my motivation. Finally, thank you to my friends and family, especially my daughter, Hollis, and my son, Mason. You continue to inspire, motivate, and push me to hustle every day!

Contents

About the Author

 **Kathey K. Porter** is a small business expert with an impressive resume that spans nearly two decades and includes work in marketing, small business development, supplier diversity, and entrepreneurship. In her capacity as a supplier diversity director and a consultant for government agencies, higher education institutions, and corporations, she has successfully helped small businesses win millions of dollars in contracts and business opportunities. In 2018, she was named Supplier Diversity Advocate of the Year by the Florida State Minority Supplier Development Council (FSMSDC). She was previously a marketing executive in the beauty industry for companies such as Carson Products, Revlon Professional, and Colomer USA, where she was responsible for new product development, launch strategies, and marketing activation for brands targeting multicultural consumers.

Porter has been the owner and operator of several businesses over the course of her career, and she is currently the CEO and principal of Porter Brown Associates, LLC (porterbrownassociates.com), a veteran-owned consultancy focusing on management and scientific and technical consulting services for government agencies, corporations, and small businesses and BusinessFAB Media, a multimedia company focusing on content for women entrepreneurs and producer of the podcast, *Becoming BusinessFAB … Fearless. Awesome. Boss.*

For over a decade, Porter has been an adjunct business instructor, lecturing at a number of colleges and universities, including the University of

Florida's Warrington College of Business, Virginia Tech's Pamplin College of Business, Savannah State University, and the Savannah College of Art and Design (SCAD), to name a few. She specializes in undergraduate and graduate classes on a variety of topics, including entrepreneurship, marketing, management, introduction to business, business ethics, public relations, business communications, leadership principles, and professional writing.

Porter's first book, *50 Billion Dollar Boss: African American Women Sharing Stories of Success in Entrepreneurship and Leadership* (Palgrave Macmillan), was nominated for the 2015 NAACP Image™ Award for Outstanding Literary Work: Non-fiction, and it ranked as a #1 new release in business and entrepreneurship on Amazon.com.

A frequent speaker, panelist, and workshop facilitator, Porter was appointed to the Florida Advisory Council on Small and Minority Business Development by the secretary for the Florida Department of Management Services, and she has served on the Task Analysis Committee for the Certified Professional in Supplier Diversity (CPSD) certification through the Institute for Supply Management (ISM).

Porter has been featured in numerous media outlets, including *Ebony*, *Black Enterprise*, the *Huffington Post*, *The Atlanta Journal-Constitution*, Sirius XM, and Fox 5 DC. She is a contributor to several local and national platforms, including the *Business in Greater Gainesville* magazine and *OPEN Forum* (American Express), and has frequently been featured as the guest small business expert in *Essence* magazine.

Porter received her MBA from Georgia Southern University, her BBA from Savannah State University, and her CPSD (Certified Professional in Supplier Diversity) credentials from the Institute for Supply Management. She also served as a supply specialist in the Georgia Army National Guard.

Porter has a daughter, Hollis, a graduate of Virginia Tech, and a son, Mason, both future entrepreneurs.

For more info, go to katheyporter.com

List of Figures

List of Tables

Part I

**Creation, Evolution, and Emergence
of Supplier Diversity Programs**

1

Supplier Diversity Programs in the Public Sector

When supplier diversity programs began, the nation was ripe for economic change and inclusion. The federal government is the largest, longest-running, and most comprehensive program for diverse businesses. However, many other industries that are part of the public sector have formalized their processes and efforts to become viable and lucrative business partners for small and diverse businesses to consider. According to Brian Tippens, noted supplier diversity expert and Director, Global Procurement Sustainability and Innovation for the Hewlett-Packard Company,

> In the United States, many companies' supplier diversity programs are built around a compliance core. These programs are designed to help ensure that the company meets compliance requirements mandated by its public sector customers. The US federal government requires that any company that provides goods and services to it, above a certain mandated minimum level, meets aggressive goals of subcontracting spend with a list of enumerated categories of underrepresented small businesses. These categories include ethnic-minority-owned, women-owned, and veteran-owned businesses.
>
> These compliance requirements have become pervasive over the past 50 years as many states, municipalities, school districts, and other public sector entities have developed supplier diversity mandates that mirror or closely reflect the U.S. federal requirements. Even companies that don't source directly to the public sector may be required to adhere to these types of requirements, if they source to other private sector companies which themselves are public sector suppliers and are required to "flow down" requirements.

© The Author(s) 2019
K. K. Porter, *Implementing Supplier Diversity*, https://doi.org/10.1007/978-3-319-94394-7_1

Depending on the industry, creating an effective supplier diversity plan in the public sector and implementing it are very different in practice. This is due to a number of factors, including internal priorities, program support and leadership, industry regulations and legislation, political climate, and historical disparities. The level at which any or all of these factors exist can directly impact the efficacy, the complexity, and the robustness of a public agency's supplier diversity program and efforts.

The above factors can also impact the requirements for doing business with a public agency, such as:

- Types of allowable certifications, which are official documents confirming the special designation of the majority ownership of a business, usually ethnicity, gender, prior or current military service, or LGBT status
- Whether set-asides or designated programs requiring a percentage of government procurement contracts be reserved for disadvantaged businesses are allowed
- Types of contracting vehicles utilized
- Level of business engagement or business outreach activity
- Level of influence on legacy policy

I have been a supplier diversity practitioner and consultant across a number of industries, including local and federal government, higher education, and corporations. While some basic tactics were transferrable across industries, I often had to refine my strategy to account for the specific industries and the culture climate in which I was working in order to achieve my desired results.

As supplier diversity overall has become a bit commoditized and, arguably, generic, many industries have sought to form their own industry-specific advocacy groups, which allows for precise insights into best practices. This has resulted in the creation of better-trained professionals, stronger advocates, and, ultimately, increased opportunities for small and diverse businesses to get engaged. Although the requirements to do business may vary, these industry sectors spend tremendous amounts of money each year and have active efforts to do business with minority- and women-owned firms, thus proving that doing business in the public sector is a very worthwhile endeavor.

Federal Government

According to the US Small Business Administration (SBA), "Purchases by military and civilian installations amount to nearly $600 billion a year, and include everything from complex space vehicles to janitorial services." When it comes to supporting diversity, the government has a certain percentage of federal contracting dollars to spend with minority-owned businesses. Targeted goals for government-wide contracting dollars spent with minority businesses across multiple categories break down according to the following percentages: small businesses (23%), women-owned small businesses (5%), small disadvantaged businesses (5%), service-disabled veteran-owned small businesses (3%), and Historically Underutilized Business Zones—HUBZones (3%).

Because it may be inefficient for the federal government to buy from small suppliers in certain cases, the system encourages their major suppliers to utilize minority businesses. Large, non-minority manufacturers can attract government contracts by building subcontracting or Tier II supplier relationships with minority-owned businesses. This demonstrates their commitment to supporting supplier diversity through their purchasing, and it helps the government meet and exceed minority spend goals. When I launched my professional services consultancy, Porter Brown Associates, I knew that I wanted to focus on the federal government. After years as a supplier diversity practitioner, I am well aware of the routine for new vendors—responding to solicitations, going to vendor events, meeting contracting officers, and so on. However, as a new firm with little to no past performance, it was still a challenge. I was trying to determine which certification we should pursue first and my strategy consultant recommended leveraging my past experience in the National Guard and get certified as a veteran-owned business. Once we received our certification, we immediately started receiving solicitations set aside for veteran-owned firms. Within six months, we were awarded our first contract, a multi-year contract valued at over $1 million.

State and Local Governments

Many local and state agencies have made doing businesses with diverse businesses a part of their overall economic development plan, often aligning their efforts and mirroring programs found in the federal government and the private sector. Further, many have adopted local preference ordinances, which allow them freedom to support local suppliers, many of whom are more likely to be diverse. This is important, as local suppliers are likely to create more jobs and stimulate purchasing at the local level. For many diverse suppliers, local and state governments are usually the first line of strategy when opting to do business with an institutional customer. This strategy often proves to be prudent, as firms can learn the process and become comfortable with the expectations required to service an institutional customer while also building the capacity needed to successfully pursue loftier opportunities.

Higher Education Institutions

The business opportunities that exist with higher education institutions are sometimes overlooked by diverse businesses. However, depending on the location and the size of the school, they can actually be a primary employer and a major economic engine within a community. Depending on whether they are a public or private institution, these educational settings are usually governed by state legislation and regulations. However, some schools operate in what I call a "quasi" manner in that they do not have full autonomy because taxpayer dollars are being used and there can be no perception of preferential treatment, but they do have some flexibility in how vigorous their supplier diversity engagement and enforcement will be.

One of the leading organizations for procurement and supplier diversity professionals in higher education is the National Association of Educational Procurement (NAEP). They have a very active and engaged supplier diversity assemblage, consisting of supplier diversity professionals from higher education institutions all over the country. The group also produces the Supplier Diversity Institute (SDI), which allows practitioners to discuss best practices and success strategies for increasing engagement and providing access to contract opportunities for diverse businesses. The SDI has become one of the leading conferences for supplier diversity professionals in higher education.

Airports

In many cities, the airport can be the epicenter of the community and a prime opportunity for small businesses. Unfortunately, opportunities with airports are another area often overlooked by businesses due to their complexity. However, airports can present big chances to do business to include opportunities in infrastructure construction, small renovation projects, concessions (including restaurants and retail stores), and advertising. Ironically, it was the proposed expansion of an airport and the actions by Atlanta Mayor Jackson at the then Hartsfield Airport (now the Atlanta Hartsfield–Jackson International Airport) that placed supplier diversity front and center, becoming a model for modern-day diverse business inclusion activities.

When considering doing business with airports, it is best to understand how the procurement process is managed. In major metropolitan markets, the local municipality may manage the day-to-day operations for the airport and have full oversight for administering contracts and procurement functions for the Federal Aviation Administration (FAA). In small markets, procurement operations are managed by the airport and are separate from the local government procurement process. Opportunities for diverse business participation with airports tend to fall under the disadvantaged business enterprise (DBE) requirements, which are discussed later. To learn more about business opportunities at specific airports, businesses may contact the airport directly, as many have supplier diversity representatives in place to ensure equitable inclusion in airport projects and that their DBE goals are being met.

The FAA recently launched the *FAA dbE Connect System*, a matchmaking system (powered by B2G Now, one of the contributors to this book) that provides organizations and businesses information connecting them to certified DBE firms and then connecting businesses to potential opportunities with airports across the country. They also partner with one of the leading advocacy groups for doing business with airports, the Airport Minority Advisory Council (AMAC).

According to its website, the Airport Minority Advisory Council (AMAC) is the only non-profit trade association dedicated to promoting the full participation of minority-owned, women-owned, and disadvantaged business enterprises (M/W/DBEs) in contracting opportunities and professional development throughout the aviation and aerospace industries. Since its inception, AMAC has been at the forefront of nearly every national policy initiative impacting the participation of disadvantaged businesses in airport contracting. AMAC also works consistently with Congress, the federal government, aviation trade associations, and others as a resource for information, education, and guidance on business and employment matters.

Transportation

As an agency within the federal government, every state has a US Department of Transportation (DOT) program which manages projects in the design, construction, and maintenance of the nation's highway system and bridges. They also administer and issue the disadvantaged business enterprise (DBE) certification. The disadvantaged business enterprise (DBE) certification program is a federal program whose purpose is to increase the participation of certified DBEs in projects funded by the US Department of Transportation and other federal sectors. In some markets, the DBE certifies airport concession DBE firms, also called ACDBEs.

Many local governments have opted to accept DBE certification in lieu of having their own certification program. The DBE regulations require state and local transportation agencies that receive DOT financial assistance to establish goals for the participation of DBEs. Each DOT-assisted state or local transportation agency is required to establish annual DBE goals, to review the scopes of anticipated large prime contracts throughout the year and to establish contract-specific DBE subcontracting goals.

Utilities

According to AAF Research, "aligning your business with a growth sector is always good strategy." There is no other industry poised for tremendous future growth than utilities. Unfortunately, due to the highly specialized nature of the industry, many diverse businesses find this industry difficult to navigate and identify direct opportunities. That does not mean the opportunities and resources for support are not there. As one of the leading states for utility legislation, California adopted General Order 156, which passed in 1988, requires California's regulated energy and telecommunications companies to annually report their percentages of contracts given to businesses owned by women, disabled veterans, and people of color ("diverse business enterprises"). In 2015, the California Public Utilities Commission updated the program to include LGBT-owned businesses. Each year they analyze the supplier diversity data reported by the companies and report findings in their Utility Supplier Diversity Report Card. The only analysis of its kind in California, this report card grades the firms on their performance and breaks down spending by diverse business category for each company. This simple combination of transparency and reporting caused total contract dollars awarded to minority- and women-owned business enterprises to balloon from $2.6 million in 1986 to $8.29 billion in 2014—without any set-asides or mandates.

The leading utilities industry resource group, the National Utilities Diversity Council, conducts research to educate and develop best practices that will promote diversity in the utilities and communications industries in the areas of governance, employment, procurement, language access/customer service, and philanthropy.

Hospitals

According to a 2012 Health Industry Distributors Association Hospital Procurement Study conducted by PricewaterhouseCoopers, outside of labor costs, the supply chain—that is, purchasing necessary goods, services, and construction—can eat the largest chunk of change out of a hospital's operating budget. Translation: it costs a lot of money to keep people healthy.

As with the other industries listed above, healthcare also has a resource and advocacy group, the Healthcare Supplier Diversity Alliance. Like the other groups, their mission is two-fold in that they work to the benefit of both industry professionals and diverse businesses alike. The core functions of the organization include:

- Work together to promote supplier diversity in the healthcare supply chain.
- Gain an understanding of how Healthcare Supplier Diversity Alliance (HSDA) subscribers incorporate supplier diversity into their business practices and how businesses may better work with these organizations.
- Attend discussions on best practices utilized by all stakeholders, including manufacturers, distributors, historically underutilized businesses, group purchasing organizations, and healthcare providers.
- Gain ideas to enhance an organization's supplier diversity initiative.
- Meet key supply chain stakeholders across the healthcare supply chain.

Jesse Moore: Director of Supplier Diversity Development, Purdue University

Although supplier diversity got its start with the federal government, it was corporate America—for-profit companies that make goods and provide services—that had the most significant impact in advancing the supplier diversity industry. These companies helped to set standards and benchmarks that drove the diversification of vendor bases by demonstrating the direct relationship among consumer purchasing, profitability, and the growth of shareholder equity. The changing demographics of the United States have driven corporations to accept the reality that they must revamp old business models and adapt to reflect the new customer base or risk losing market share. Census data predict that by 2044, the majority of the population of the United States will be made up of what we now classify as minority groups. With an increase in diverse populations comes an increase in buying power. That fact has captured corporate America's attention and has driven corporate leaders to diversify their workforce as well as their supplier bases. Many agencies within the public sector have taken notice of this trend and are actively seeking to take their respective programs to the next level, emulating many of the tactics that corporations use to engage and utilize diverse businesses.

For the past 13 years, I was the director of supplier diversity development at Purdue University in West Lafayette, Indiana. I was recruited to initiate Purdue's formal supplier diversity program, though, initially, Purdue's human resources department informed me that I would not be considered for the position because I did not have a purchasing background. Purdue was about to embark upon the same path taken by most universities and colleges that start a supplier diversity program: assign this responsibility to a low- to mid-level procurement professional, on top of that person's other daily duties. To that point, my professional career had centered around business advocacy with various chambers of commerce and state economic development organizations. Luckily for me, Purdue was open to bucking the status quo in higher education, and they gave me the opportunity to lead a new approach. Together, we began an award-winning program that has been successful for Purdue and, more importantly, has contributed to the success of countless minority businesses.

By state statute, public institutions in Indiana must submit a report on diversity spend each November to the Governor's Commission on Women and Minority Business Enterprises. This is the entity that oversees Indiana's supplier diversity program. According to the most recent report (November 2017), Purdue's contract spending with diverse firms totaled $84 million, a $29 million increase over the previous year's spend. The report submitted in 2006 showed the total spend at $28 million. Here are four key factors that contributed to our success.

Created Partnerships in the Process. The first and most important factor was that Purdue decided to deviate from the norm and hire a business advocate with experience in the marketplace. This allowed me to develop a strategic plan that focused on three major areas: internal staff development and partnerships, external outreach, and marketing and communications.

Internal staff development and partnerships: We first sought to educate staff and the campus community at large about what supplier diversity meant, about how their actions contributed to the program's success and helped perpetuate supplier diversity, and about the importance of making diverse vendors "top of mind" companies when making purchasing decisions. We established inter-campus strategic partnerships between our business managers and various departments (i.e., procurement, contracting, and physical facilities) to ensure that they were all engaged and enlisted to recognize where diverse firms could be introduced to opportunities. We also facilitated events and introductions to provide valuable face time between our teams and potential vendors.

External outreach: We placed heavy emphasis on getting to the farthest reaches of the state to spread the word about the opportunities at Purdue for qualified, diverse firms. We participated in vendors' fairs, coordinated panel discussions with the seven state educational institutions (SEIs), and created special events that brought the Purdue University Physical Facilities staff to Indianapolis each June to share upcoming projects and to meet with construction and construction-related firms. One of the events, Construction Connection, included other SEIs and select private construction projects to make them aware of Purdue's program and to give them an opportunity to ask questions. We plan and conduct monthly meetings for qualified diverse firms to meet with other larger employers in our Greater Lafayette community. We also believe that it is important to network with other supplier diversity professionals both in higher education and in corporate America, and to that end we became actively involved with two national organizations: National Association of Educational Procurement (NAEP) and the National Minority Supplier Development Council (NMSDC). Purdue recognizes the value in interacting with and learning from other supplier diversity professionals, whether in education (e.g., NAEP) or in corporate America (e.g., NMSDC).

Marketing and communications: We use our website and our newsletters, *The Catalyst* and *The Starfish*, to communicate with the public about Purdue's supplier diversity program and the many activities in which we are involved. We include links on our website to many other strategic resources, all of which make it their mission to assist diverse businesses. *The Catalyst* is a quarterly newsletter written for external audiences. It has current news about the university's purchasing and contracting processes, in addition to local and national news that impacts small diverse businesses. *The Starfish* is an internal-only newsletter used to introduce staff to diverse firms that have been awarded contracts to provide products or services to the university. We believe that if staff see that we have done our due diligence and that the firms are on campus or have recently completed work for Purdue, then some of the fears associated with trying a new supplier might be allayed. We always include a testimonial from a Purdue staffer, along with that person's contact information, so that potential customers can gain further information as needed.

Leadership Sent a Clear Message to the Staff. The university assigned the supplier diversity function to the Purdue Office of the Executive Vice President and Treasurer, which made it clear to internal staff and external constituents that supplier diversity was important to the top administrators and the board of trustees. This gave the program immediate access to deans, department heads, chamber presidents, affinity group leadership, legislators, business community leaders, and other vital stakeholders.

Dedicated Focus. When the vast majority of higher education institutions begin a supplier diversity initiative or program, a procurement staffer is typically charged with managing the new program under "other duties as assigned." This places tremendous pressure on that staff person to fulfill both the procurement and supplier diversity roles, and the priority is usually given to procurement responsibilities. Such an approach allows an institution to "check the box" about having a supplier diversity program, but those programs often have uneven outcomes. When Purdue made the decision to engage in supplier diversity, they wanted a full-time staffer who could focus exclusively on building and maintaining the university's supplier diversity program.

Accountability Is Critical. Our program enjoys active and visible support from top administrators and from the board of trustees, and Purdue provided me with sufficient resources for a viable budget, for implementation of the strategic plan, and for the hiring of necessary staff to ensure that we have the administrative bandwidth needed to carry out the strategic plan.

Indiana has a database called ConnXus, which was created to introduce state firms to other companies in Indiana that can fulfill contracts before taking those contracts outside of the state. The unintended consequence was the creation of the largest database of women- and minority-owned firms in Indiana. ConnXus is a free resource that easily answers the oft-asked question, "Where *are* diverse firms in Indiana?" We also developed an event to bring diverse firms onto campus to meet with decision makers. We named it "Relationships to Partnerships" in order to drive home the fact that this event was meant to be the starting point for building business relationships that could ultimately lead to securing a contract; it was not an automatic awarding of contracts. The event has grown over the years, and today 12 local large firms send their decision makers to the gathering, which adds value to the visiting diverse firms and allows local firms to meet with many qualified entrepreneurs. The event has the support of companies like Caterpillar Inc., Fifth Third Bank, Wabash National, Oerlikon Fairfield, Indiana University Health, Kirby Risk, Alcoa, Greater Lafayette Commerce, the City of Lafayette, and the City of West Lafayette. Additionally, Tippecanoe County commissioners sign an annual joint proclamation with the mayors of Lafayette and West Lafayette declaring the date of our event Supplier Diversity Day. I am proud to say that November 2017 marked the event's 13th year. It is deeply gratifying to have been a part of Purdue's efforts to increase diversity spend at the university.

I would be remiss if I did not mention the single most influential event that has impacted our success at Purdue. In 2014, the Indiana legislature passed a law that authorized Indiana's SEIs to utilize construction managers as constructors (CMc) as a delivery tool for new construction projects. This law now allows SEIs to negotiate individual elements of a construction project such as cost, time, safety, and diversity. Without dictating the diversity spend with the contractors, Purdue has required each one to include a utilization plan that will be considered in final selection. This new tool accounts for the majority of the $29 million increase year over year in our diversity spend. This law and Purdue's staff's willingness to maximize its usage has significant potential to boost the total dollars won by diverse firms in the future.

Like most universities, we are tasked with balancing the challenges of implementing an effective supplier diversity program with the squeeze of controlling the cost of an education at Purdue. Our president, Mitch Daniels, is leading this charge nationally. We firmly believe that the motivation for starting a supplier diversity program would not be because it "feels good." Diverse businesses must add value to the university to win a contract. Studies conducted by corporations regularly show that these programs benefit corporate America and that they are a wise return on investment, which is why so many corporations have supplier diversity programs. Higher education institutions are slowly realizing that corporate America is ahead of the curve when it comes to supplier diversity programs. It is only a matter of time before higher education institutions catch up and fully embrace supplier diversity development.

2

Supplier Diversity Programs in the Private Sector: Corporations

Corporations are beginning to use supply chain management as a strategy for increasing profitability, growth, cost containment, and customer value. Supply chain management and supplier diversity share benefits such as enriched reputation, competitive advantage, morale boosting, and innovation; stakeholder relations also accrue from both supplier diversity initiatives which have demonstrated a direct impact on consumer purchasing decisions, whereas historically they were presumed to have an indirect impact. This means that such initiatives also have return-on-investment potential. Firms need both resource capital and institutional capital for a long-run competitive advantage, and future research should study the combined effects of both as a source of competitive advantage for firms.

When looking beyond finances to social responsibility, supplier diversity is often seen as a testament to a company's commitment to producing a socially responsible impact in local communities. Supplier diversity programs also meet customer mandates, leverage governmental initiatives, and comply with federal supplier requirements. By making strategic use of supplier relationships to reach procurement goals, organizations can maximize their supply chain potential.

Supplier Diversity = Supplier Relationship Management

Supplier relationship management (SRM) identifies and engages the right stakeholders to create ownership of the relationship, drive effective communication, and align strategic objectives. The result is a foundation for continuous

© The Author(s) 2019
K. K. Porter, *Implementing Supplier Diversity*, https://doi.org/10.1007/978-3-319-94394-7_2

efficiency improvements, such as cost reductions, risk mitigation or improved go-to-market times, and arguably, most importantly, an improved potential for disruptive innovation. Interestingly, the ideologies of supplier relationship management closely resemble those of supplier diversity.

It is no secret that organizations must assess every aspect of their business in order to achieve any level of a competitive edge. When it comes to the supply chain, what leaders are embracing and pushing as supplier relationship management, supplier diversity has been preaching and practicing for years. As supplier diversity lead with the University of Florida (UF), in partnership with our procurement department, I created a three-pronged approach to supplier relationship management called *Connect–Engage–Buy*. This was the underpinning of our program on which I created business development workshops, learning opportunities, and events that would provide the most benefit to firms looking to do business with the University. The program included:

CONNECT—Connect with the organization and program, that is, registering as a vendor.
ENGAGE—Engage in the program offerings and events to make connections and build relationships.
BUY—Learn what and how departments buy various goods and services.

Also, diverse and small businesses that were new to doing business with the University of Florida were encouraged to participate in our mentor-protégé program, a year-long program which allowed them to be mentored by a larger firm with extensive experience doing business with the University and provided unfettered access to their key personnel, operations, and resources. By building a relationship over the course of a year, firms emerged stronger and better prepared to do business, not just with UF but wherever there were business opportunities.

Our program was designed to help minority- and women-owned businesses grow in a way that enabled them to develop a position of strength in the marketplace. Our investment in building these relationships trains businesses to succeed in the future, crafting a sustainable economic platform that creates jobs, promotes increased economic activity, and generates innovation.

A Deloitte study on supplier relationship management suggests the need for organizations to look beyond traditional procurement-centric perspectives on supplier management and explore how relationships with key partners can be managed in a more strategic and holistic manner. Despite the trend to compress and simplify the supply chain, consequently, relying on fewer suppliers (often leaving diverse suppliers out of the supply chain), globalization increases organizational complexity and risk, thus requiring increased specialization and collaboration at many levels and from various functions. More than ever, executives are looking for innovative ways to leverage existing and new supplier relationships in support of their growth and/or expansion pursuits.

Deloitte's 2014 Global Chief Procurement Officer (CPO) Survey found increasing levels of supplier collaboration and restructuring of existing relationships among the top procurement levels. While in some industries, 77% of CPOs may be actively driving innovation with suppliers, the vast majority view the effectiveness of their strategic supplier collaborations as poor or mixed. Although this is speculation, I predict these are also organizations with little to no supplier diversity efforts. Conversely, a strong supplier diversity program and outreach efforts provide the foundation for a strong SRM program. The most successful organizations use SRM to drive all activities regarding supplier management. SRM is not only deployed as a tool in special circumstances or used only on a certain sections of the supplier base. Rather, it is used across the company and across the entire supply base.

Deloitte, one of world's leading supplier relationship management consultants, outlines the benefits that companies derive from successfully managing SRM efforts:

Reduced costs. Beyond traditional sourcing and category management efforts across the entire supply chain through the continual optimization of operations in a win-win partnership with suppliers

Increased performance. Of strategic suppliers in a transparent manner maintaining focus on key measures that support business objectives

Better management of supply risk and compliance. Through responsible sourcing, ethics, and regulatory requirements

Improved business development and innovation. By jointly identifying and implementing opportunities that create long-term value for both organizations

A 2012 study by CAPS Research, a nonprofit research center for procurement and supply management leadership, indicated that 71.79% of organizations expected their total supplier diversity program spend to increase in the coming years. An article in *Supply & Demand Chain Executive* magazine indicated that in 2011, AT&T spent $12 billion with diverse suppliers, surpassing its corporate goal—21.5% of its total spend with certified diverse businesses by 2012—one year ahead of schedule. Others, such as transportation and supply chain management solutions provider Ryder System Inc., are recognized by major manufacturers like Toyota Motor Engineering & Manufacturing, North America, Inc. (TEMA) for their minority business enterprise (MBE) development efforts. Some reach even higher diversity spending goals. The Kellogg Company, for example, spent $353 million on goods and services from diverse, first-tier suppliers in 2011.

So what's driving this added spotlight to supplier diversity programs? A 2011 Institute for Supply Management (ISM) Supplier Diversity Survey indicates:

- 76.9% of companies justify having a supplier diversity program because "it's the right thing to do."
- 61.1% of companies cite federal reporting regulations as another core reason.
- 59.8% confirm that since their customers are diverse, their businesses should also be diverse.

According to Elizabeth A. Vazquez, president, CEO, and co-founder of WEConnect International, a global women's entrepreneurship advocacy group based in Washington, DC, "The interest in supplier diversity is coming from a lot of different directions. The fact that Dun and Bradstreet shone a light on what is possible, what the obstacles are and what some of the best solutions are in effectively implementing a supplier diversity program is critical because not all corporations understand its full value proposition throughout the organization. It has to start at the top. The top folks have to embrace it and then the ones who are responsible for implementing it have to have the resources to be able to sell it throughout the organization, track and measure it and ultimately earn the recognition for the good work that they are doing."

Tailoring Programs to Meet the Needs of the Organization

Like the public sector, organizational approaches to supplier diversity program can come in a variety of forms depending on the objectives, core business, and complexities of the organization. Here, we highlight two different examples of supplier diversity programs in vastly different industries—a mature supplier diversity program with General Motors and a fairly new program with Google.

GM Grows Its Own Diverse Suppliers

General Motors' supplier diversity program was launched in 1968, after race riots in Detroit a year earlier left 43 people dead and hundreds injured. The idea was to help provide jobs for the local community. According to Linda Ware, supplier diversity manager for Global Purchasing and Supply Chain for GM, the company provided loans to businesses near GM's headquarters in the hope that those businesses would use the money to hire diverse employees from the community.

By the early 1990s, the program had evolved into a full-fledged supplier diversity initiative aimed at developing, providing loans to GM minority- and women-owned business enterprise (MWBE) suppliers. Today, more than 200 minority- and women-owned businesses supply GM. While GM obviously sought to provide social benefits through the diversity program, the company also envisioned the program as an opportunity to expand its customer base. The hope was that diverse suppliers in GM's network would hire employees who would in turn purchase vehicles from GM in gratitude for supporting the community.

Networking and training is another area on which GM places a lot of emphasis. Interestingly, the two components are so intermingled that one seldom occurs without the other. Networking occurs in two ways: MWBE suppliers mingling with company executives, managers, and community members; and MWBE suppliers networking with each other. These activities also give potential MWBE suppliers a chance to meet a variety of influential people like MWBE council members and representatives from community stakeholder/support organizations. Additionally, potential Tier I and Tier II suppliers can mingle with current GM diverse suppliers and get inside information on the procurement process. GM also encourages suppliers who hope to land a GM contract to mingle with each other and exchange innovative ideas that MWBE businesses have used for growth and greater market access outside GM.

Because developing a pipeline of minority and women suppliers is important for continued success, accessibility to training is critical. GM works closely with MWBE suppliers to ensure they understand the procurement process and what is required to get on the bid list, understanding that it can take years from initial supplier contact with GM before the vendor is added to the list of eligible Tier I or Tier II suppliers. It is then Ware's job to ensure that they actually get included.

Google's Unique Business Required a Unique Approach to Supplier Diversity

While Google is an engineering-centric business that develops many of its new products in-house, like other major corporations, it outsources services and products that do not fit within its core competency, such as food and transportation. This is where diverse suppliers bring a number of tools to the table as value chain partners and Google was ready to introduce these businesses to the Google way. Launched in 2014, Google's program was designed to:

- Connect more Google employees with diverse-owned small suppliers
- Connect diverse businesses to opportunities within Google
- Help those suppliers grow on the Web and improve their business skills, and, finally
- Foster innovation at the supply chain level

Since its inception, Google has sought to take a different approach to developing its supplier diversity program, eschewing many of the traditional supplier diversity program models. One of the ways that they achieved this is that it opted not to require certification for women- or minority-owned businesses. Staying close to its roots, the application process was designed to be comprehensive, yet accessible and simple. By not restricting participation to certified small businesses, Google opened the door to working with a wider variety of diverse-owned businesses. The program is open to all historically underutilized businesses, including minority-owned, women-owned, LGBT-owned, disabled-owned, and veteran-owned businesses, as long as they meet the established criteria.

Another reason that supplier diversity at Google is different is that procurement works differently, especially in relation to comparably sized companies. Procurement does not work in the traditional manner—there is no formal or centralized procurement function and it does not make buying decisions. While Google's Procure to Pay (P2P) team owns and maintains the procurement processes and systems, Googlers, all 65,000 of them, are empowered to make their own purchasing decisions, based on their specific needs. This open approach, coupled with encouragement to do business with a broad spectrum of suppliers, helps to ensure that innovations being developed outside of Google can get noticed and be given a fair shot at becoming an element of Google's value proposition—an integrator of technology and a provider of cutting-edge digital services.

With a model so different from how vendors are used to working and have been working for years, how does Google learn about and gain access to a broad spectrum of suppliers, especially diverse suppliers? Answering that very question became the catalyst for Google to create one of the most innovating supplier diversity program entries in years.

Initially, Google was working on a "business inclusion" initiative, looking at the diversity of its customer base and the diversity of its workforce, not necessarily the diversity of its supply chain. However, they began to realize that if they wanted small and diverse businesses as customers, they should also want them as suppliers. According to Adrianna Samaniego, senior global program manager of Google's Small Business Supplier Diversity program, "We worked to be truly open for business and have economic impact."

At the time, Google was considered a "black box" to small and diverse suppliers—perceived as mysterious or even inaccessible. Similarly, small and diverse suppliers were not easily accessible for Googlers. With no formal supplier selection process, Googlers often learned of suppliers by word of mouth or from colleagues. Further, to even get listed on Google's internal corporate supplier registration site required a supplier to already have a contact inside the company. Finding that contact required patience, persistence, and, sometimes, a little luck. "One small business spent two and a half years asking around at our bus stop areas for the right person to talk to about their company before they found a contact," Samaniego says. This is an extreme example, but it demonstrates the tremendous lengths businesses had to go to in order to pitch their services.

The team researched what constituted a best-in-class supplier diversity program, starting with its peers in high tech. At the time, they were surprised to learn that other than Intel and Dell, few had formal programs (others have since started programs). They also looked at how the certification processes worked with leading organizations such as the National Minority Supplier Development Council (NMSDC) and the Women's Business Enterprise National Council (WBENC) and what was happening with the federal government.

Google also reached out to the business community across the United States to hear what diverse-owned small businesses wanted and needed. There were several key learnings. One was that suppliers did not want to spend hours completing applications, updating certifications, or mining through complicated portals. They simply wanted a foot in the door.

Second, for many small businesses, marketing is not always viewed as a necessity but more of a luxury. The dilemma became convincing these businesses that investing in Google products, that is, their Web presence as a marketing tool, would yield a return. Businesses liked the idea of growing their digital skills so that they could ensure they would have an equitable opportunity to participate in today's online economy but just did not know quite where or how to start. All of this feedback further influenced the way the Google team went about designing their program.

Once they had the framework for their program, Google determined that the next step would be to include a business development program and partnered with the Tuck School of Business at Dartmouth College. The Tuck School has deep expertise in the structure and management of supply chains. But they have also become known for their unique expertise in developing diverse suppliers and helping them scale and grow their businesses. Since 1980, Tuck has been providing custom learning experiences tailored to the needs of minority business owners. Google opted to create a series of short, bootcamp programs, with none lasting longer than a week. The design of these programs reflects the fact that the typical entrepreneur knows the technical side of their business, whether it is manufacturing a product or delivering a service. It is on the business side and setting up the systems necessary to support a robust supply chain like Google, where they need the most support. It might sound a bit self-serving, but let's face it; poorly run businesses are not good supply chain partners.

Since Google was founded in 1998, digital information has become central to how a business is controlled, and how customers and suppliers interact with the business. Google has a broad array of business tools available to make suppliers more effective and efficient by accessing and analyzing information. As Google and their parent company, Alphabet, continue to expand into almost every industry imaginable—hardware, self-driving cars, health, shopping, and so on—they understand that in order to continue to be innovative, their supply chain needs to be inclusive.

Supply Chain Sustainability Through Strategic Supplier Inclusion

Diversity involves recognizing all the ways people are different from each other, including everything that makes each individual unique. Inclusion expands on this premise by combining and using these diverse forces and resources in ways that benefit the organization to create a culture of inclusion. While many corporations have come to learn that both diversity and inclusion are needed in order for their organizations to survive, many forward-thinking supplier diversity practitioners are also embracing the principles of inclusion and applying them to their programs. According to ConnXus, while many business leaders readily view diversity as a positive influence on corporate thinking, not enough have realized that inclusion can actually result in a stronger corporate culture and image and better business decisions and results.

Inspiring Next-Level Thinking About Inclusion

When firms are ready to move beyond just "checking the boxes" for supplier diversity categories and implementing supplier inclusion programs, ConnXus provides five proven tips on assessing and creating an action plan:

- Make sure diverse suppliers are included in sourcing lists from the beginning.
- Choose sourcing strategies that align with organizational supplier diversity strategies.
- After hosting solicitation events, negotiate aggressively with minority-owned suppliers—so both parties' needs are fulfilled.
- Develop supplier management and integration metrics in advance, to ensure successful and sustainable inclusion.
- Conduct "readiness assessments" with supplier diversity partners before entering into new supply chain arrangements.

Part II

Driving Entrepreneurship

3

Impact of Supplier Diversity on Startup Activity and Small Business Growth

According to the Chartered Institute of Procurement & Supply (CIPS), "Supplier development is the process of working with certain suppliers on a one-to-one basis to improve their performance (and capabilities) for the benefit of the buying organization and can take the form of a one-off project or an on-going activity that may take some years to come to fruition." Forward-thinking companies are leading the way in multicultural marketplaces by infusing supplier diversity into their main business processes in unique and creative ways. Many of those who have developed strong relationships with minority business owners are reaping the benefits.

When supplier diversity began, it was a new frontier for everyone. Organizations and entrepreneurs alike learned as they went. The focus was very transactional, and companies used basic metrics to quantify their success. In their quest to report on quick metrics, companies used a process that looked something like this: direct firms to register, wait for opportunities, submit a bid, wait for a response, repeat. However, as supplier diversity grew in complexity and programs shifted from executive order to entrenched business strategy, organizations began to integrate their programs further into the fabric of their respective cultures. Senior leadership started demanding to see how they were doing, requiring more sophisticated metrics in order to justify the resources used to support the program.

Companies also began to realize the value of focusing on facilitating business success. According to CVM Solutions, developing suppliers puts them into position for improvement and additional success. The benefits of having a development program are immense, as these programs can help diverse suppliers strengthen their business processes and profit margins, become certified

© The Author(s) 2019
K. K. Porter, *Implementing Supplier Diversity*, https://doi.org/10.1007/978-3-319-94394-7_3

with appropriate agencies, and cement themselves as trusted partners within the organization's supply chain. Supplier development ultimately increases diverse spending and reduces the amount of time spent seeking new suppliers, because most of those signing a contract with the organization are not likely to leave if they are making progress in building relationships and growing their business. In this way, supplier development begets more organizational success, which begets more supplier development.

A 2014 study commissioned by the National Minority Supplier Development Council (NMSDC) and conducted by the Institute for Thought Diversity sought to assess the economic impact that the NMSDC minority business enterprise community has on the US economy (and Puerto Rico). This impact included the increased business activity created by the nearly 12,000 NMSDC-certified minority business enterprises (MBEs), the jobs that are maintained/created as a result of this activity throughout the various sectors of the US economy, and the incremental business taxes that are generated as a result.

The study illustrated that NMSDC-certified MBEs have a total economic impact of over $400 billion in output, which resulted in the creation and/or preservation of more than 2.2 million jobs held by persons who find themselves either directly or indirectly employed by NMSDC-certified MBEs. These are jobs that not only support individuals, but also contribute to the economic well-being of their families, their communities, and the nation. Further, these suppliers generated close to $49 billion in tax revenue for the benefit of local, state, and federal governments.

In no other city has the positive impact supplier diversity initiatives can have on minority businesses been demonstrated more than in Atlanta, Georgia. In 1974, Maynard Jackson, the newly elected Mayor of Atlanta, set out to challenge Atlanta's GOB (good 'ole boy) network and negotiated a deal with city business leaders mandating that 25% of construction contracts be set aside for businesses of color. At the time, this was unheard of and it did not come without its challenges. Some even called it illegal, insisting that the governor and state legislators seize control of the airport. After a two-year battle, the old guard relented and agreed to the set-aside plan. The results were electric. In less than five years, contracts to minority firms increased from less than 1% the year prior to just under 40%. Unbeknownst at the time, Jackson was creating history. This initiative directly supported historically marginalized businesses, invested in communities, and Jackson's efforts empowered the black middle class. Additionally, these efforts helped create many black millionaires and produce many of *Black Enterprise* magazine's BE 100 s companies, many of which are still in operation today, and cementing Atlanta's status as a mecca for black entrepreneurship. Most importantly, it became a model of what could happen with strong leaders and champions of supplier diversity and sparked development in other major cities, including Chicago, Detroit, Los Angeles, and Boston. In 2009, the late Herman Russell, chairman/CEO of the Atlanta construction company HJ Russell, a direct beneficiary of this new policy and an annual stalwart on the BE 100 list, told *Black Enterprise* that his then $300 million company would not have been that size if not for Jackson's policy.

The impact of Jackson's mandates continues today, with more than $1.6 billion, or 37%, of Atlanta's Hartfield Jackson Airport's (which was subsequently named after Jackson in 2003) construction, remodeling, runway expansion, and concessions contracts being awarded to diverse businesses. Additionally, Atlanta consistently ranks as one of the top cities for business by people of color.

Michele Hoskins: CEO, Michele Foods

I started Michele Foods in the early 1980s with one product: a pancake syrup made from a generations-old family recipe from my great-great-grandmother. Today, my family business has several products that are sold in more than 10,000 stores nationwide. I have been featured in in dozens of newspapers and magazines, including *Essence, Black Enterprise, People, Fortune*, and even the *National Enquirer*. And my proverbial rags-to-riches story has been spotlighted three times in what has become the pinnacle of all media for letting people know that you've made it: *The Oprah Winfrey Show*.

Everything I did when I was getting Michele Foods started was unconventional. I admit that there were times when I did not have the answer or know what my next move would be, but I can recall three very distinct periods where supplier diversity programs helped my business scale and propel to the next level.

From the Basement to the Shelf

In the early days, we were filling the syrup bottles in my mother's basement. I had a co-packer who would make the syrup and fill a 55-gallon drum that would be delivered to the basement. I purchased bottles and caps and had a supplier make labels. Every evening, my routine was to use a funnel to fill the bottles (after I made sure everything was sterilized, of course). It would take three to four hours to fill a case. The next day, I would take the filled cases to all of the neighborhood grocery stores on Chicago's South Side. At the time, I did not even have a pricing strategy. I just asked the store manager if I could put the product on the shelf. I was mainly selling on consignment. If any syrup sold, I would invoice the stores. If none sold, I would go back and get the product. For a time, I would go in and buy the syrup myself and have my family and friends do the same. But I knew that was not a sustainable model and not the type of business that I envisioned. I wanted Michele Foods to be a household name and to be in thousands of stores across the country.

After six months, I got my product into several grocery stores, about 48 in total, all of them mom-and-pop stores in predominantly African American communities. At the time, there were not many African American–owned food products. When I went in and requested shelf space, no one knew what to say, so no one turned me down. I'd put the syrup on the shelf and just hoped that it would sell.

After a few years, I decided that it was time to grow again. I decided to approach Jewel Food Stores and Dominick's. I knew that I needed a new strategy for approaching Jewel and Dominick's, and I was emboldened by something I'd read in the newspaper. At the time, a Dominick's was being built on 79th Street on the South Side. Jesse Jackson had been picketing and told them, "If you're going to put this Dominick's in a Black community, you've got to bring in Black products." During that time, there were numerous African American entrepreneurs making hair care or household cleaning products, but few, if any, made food products. This was the perfect opportunity for me to introduce them to my company. I may not have been aware of the details as an outsider looking in, but I knew that there was a movement afoot and I wanted to get in on the ground floor.

Becoming a Regional Product

I made an appointment to meet with the buyer for Jewel Food Stores in Melrose Park, a Chicago suburb. Initially, they tried to steer me to human resources, as if I was there for a job, but I assured them that I was in the right place. When I finally met with the buyer, he told me that he had been a buyer with Jewel for 35 years and had never ever seen a woman with a product that she owned, let alone an African American woman. Normally, he was called on by salesmen or saleswomen selling national brands for major corporations. For whatever reason, my assertiveness worked. He told me that if his grandson liked my syrup, he would give me a shot. A couple of days went by, and he called me back. He said his grandson loved it, and he would put it in Jewel Food Stores! The first order was for 672 cases of syrup. And I was able to get into Dominick's soon after.

Getting into Jewel and Dominick's introduced my product to a whole new consumer, and people of all races were soon choosing my product over others. As much as I wanted to believe that I got into the stores because my syrup was so good, I realized that neither of the stores needed another syrup on their shelves. The truth was that I was someone they could hold up as an example of their inclusiveness and social responsibility. I was a diversity tool for Jewel and Dominick's. Over the years, I would become more familiar with diversity initiatives, and eventually I learned how to use them to my advantage.

When I first started, I focused largely on grocery stores. Most of us think that grocery stores—and all retail stores for that matter—are in the business of selling goods to consumers, but they are actually in the business of real estate. Except for private labels and store-owned brands, retailers do not own the products on their shelves. They rent the shelf space out to the manufacturers that own the products. Whenever a retail product goes onto a shelf, the store assesses a fee for that space, called a slotting charge. Some manufacturers may pay upward of several thousands of dollars in fees for their shelf space. On top of the slotting fee, the retailer takes a percentage of the sale of every product, anywhere from 15% to 35%. An item's turnover, or how much it sells, is very important because that determines whether the store is making money from that item. Because both Jewel and Dominick's wanted a relationship with me, an African American–owned and women-owned business, they waived their slotting fees. This allowed me to maximize my few resources in order to make a go of this window of opportunity.

I remained a regional product for nine years. I had gotten into a comfortable groove with Jewel and Dominick's and was on a roll. We expanded our consumer base and were appealing to general market consumers. We interacted with consumers at local events and handed out samples everywhere we went. We offered in-store demonstrations, where we made countless pancakes served with Michele's Honey Crème Syrup. But here was the problem: we were sticky with syrup and caked in pancake batter, but we could not get the "dough" to stick around. Something had to change.

Doing Business with Denny's and Walmart

I had experienced some success with diversity programs, and by all appearances, I was living the dream, with a product in 900 stores across the Midwest. But it was becoming increasingly apparent that even though they had given me the opportunity, no one but me cared that I was not making any money. I was working as hard as I could, giving everything I had to keep the product on the shelves, but I was not making much profit. So I decided to figure out why.

One day I was speaking about my dilemma with a colleague and I asked, "How do Aunt Jemima and the others make money?" He told me the big competitors sold in volume all over the country. He said I needed more orders. I know it sounds simple, but it was like a light switch had been turned on. I realized that I had settled into a comfort zone, spending all of those years in the Midwest because it was a region that I knew. I could see my products or meet with the buyers whenever I wanted or needed to.

In late 1990, I started a new weekly routine that would last for about a year and a half. Around 10:30 a.m. every Monday morning, I called Flagstar, the parent company of Denny's Restaurants. They resisted me from day one, but I was determined to do business with them. One day I opened the newspaper and read that Denny's was in hot water due to a racial discrimination case brought against them. It was horrendous episode where African American consumers were asked to prepay for their meals. I knew this could be the break that I needed, and I figured Denny's would finally see me. Because they were in such a high-profile situation, they might need someone like me.

As a result of the scandal, Flagstar cleaned house in their upper ranks so they could begin restructuring the company in the wake of the discrimination suits. Their new president, Jim Adamson, learned that I had been relentlessly pursuing business with Denny's to no avail. He realized that the company needed to get back on track and get some good press, and he began asking why there weren't a significant number of minority suppliers servicing the restaurant chain. The previous procurement executives had insisted that there were none to be found—even though I had been banging at their door for a year and a half.

When Mr. Adamson learned about my constant calling, he asked how they had responded to me. They told him that they requested samples, but somehow they were unable to find them. Once they located my samples, he called me in for a meeting. After several meetings and conversations, he decided that he wanted to give me some business, but they needed me to develop a recipe that would work for them, one that would be cost effective and that could be transported for a reasonable amount of money. I knew that this could be a huge opportunity and any misstep could be costly, so I decided to hire an industry consultant to help me create a recipe especially for Denny's. Once we got the recipe properly formulated, got good deals on raw ingredients, and found a local co-packer to manufacture the syrup, I was able to develop a satisfactory price point for Denny's. Our terms were accepted and, after a year and a half, I signed a $3 million contract with Denny's. At the time, our contract was one of Denny's first big deals with a minority-owned firm. For us, it was our biggest deal yet, and it gave me the kind of cash flow that I had only dreamed about during those nine years of struggle. Talk about a sweet deal!

While my company was experiencing its first major success, I was anxious, excited, and motivated to keep it going. One day, WGN-Channel 9 called and asked me to do a segment about the syrup with my family. We prepared a feast of fried chicken and waffles and a variety of other foods that went well with Michele's Honey Crème Syrup. After the segment aired, someone from Walmart called WGN and asked about me. They spoke with the reporter who had done the story, and he got in touch with me.

The guy's name was Wayne Easterling, and he was the diversity coordinator and manager of Walmart's Minority & Women-Owned Business Development program. His job was to go out and find people like me that he could groom as Walmart suppliers. I went to the Walmart headquarters and met with several people who told me about a couple of programs they had in place to get my product on their shelves. One of them was a diversity program called Made in America. At the time, Walmart was an aggressively growing retail chain. They realized that they had a very diverse set of people coming through their doors to buy a very diverse set of products. With all of the increasing talk about diversity, Walmart was not taking their program lightly.

Walmart was also a proponent of American might. Their "Made in America" slogan supported and promoted domestically made products. A product had to be produced in America to get into Walmart. That meant that your item had to be manufactured by American labor and with raw materials produced within the United States. It was not hard for me to qualify for the diversity program because my company was 100% minority owned. The "Made in America" criteria were a breeze too because everything I bought was American produced. So Walmart put my products on shelves in some of their stores. That was another big deal for my company, but more importantly, Walmart helped me achieve a bigger goal, which was to expand out of my comfort zone.

While I had the determination to grow my business at any cost, I am not sure whether my results would have been the same had it not been for some lucky timing and my engagement with supplier diversity programs.

4

The State of Diverse Suppliers

For many, entrepreneurship *is* the American Dream. Everyone loves a good "bootstrapping" story and nothing demonstrates that more effectively than taking an idea and turning it into a growing, thriving enterprise and creating wealth for the entrepreneur and employees. For millions of Americans, starting and owning a business has been the route to success, security, and providing for one's community. This is particularly true for people of color, who face disparate unemployment rates and obstacles breaking through the "good old boys network" to secure good, stable jobs.

An economic downturn or recession might not seem like the most opportune time to start a business, but depending on the type of business, a recession can actually be the ideal time to take the plunge and launch a new company. In fact, many well-known and successful organizations were born during an economic slump:

- Hyatt Corp. opened its first hotel's doors at the Los Angeles International Airport during the Eisenhower recession (1957–1958).
- Burger King Corp. started in 1954 during another recession. During another recession in 1957, the company introduced its successful signature burger—the Whopper.
- IHOP Corp. also opened its doors in July 1958 during the Eisenhower recession.
- Wikipedia Foundation Inc. was born during the post-9/11 recession.
- GE (General Electric Co.) was established in 1876 by the famed American inventor Thomas Edison. In the middle of the Panic of 1873, a six-year

© The Author(s) 2019
K. K. Porter, *Implementing Supplier Diversity*, https://doi.org/10.1007/978-3-319-94394-7_4

recession, Edison created one of the best-known inventions of all time—the incandescent light bulb.
* HP (Hewlett-Packard Development Company LP) was inauspiciously born at the end of the Great Depression.

Yes, these are extreme examples of wildly successful brands who likely had no idea of the level of success they would go on to achieve. The 2007 economic downturn demonstrated how communities of color utilized entrepreneurship to remain resilient in times of crisis. In fact, from 2007 to 2012, the number of minority-owned businesses increased by 38%, while non-minority businesses decreased by 6%.

Despite its inherent challenges, this is an exciting time to be an entrepreneur and, more specifically, a supplier. Successful disability-, LGBTQ-, minority-, veteran-, and women-owned businesses can achieve even more success by partnering with companies looking to increase supplier diversity programs. Many organizations indicate that increasing their relationships with diverse companies has become a priority for them, but it can be a struggle to form those partnerships. This situation can be especially frustrating for vendors who are ready to expand their businesses but fail to capture the attention of companies that can benefit from their services.

A Demographic Shift

In 2002, a Minority Business Development Agency (MBDA) Survey of Business Owners suggested that, by 2025, the minority population will exceed the non-minority population in five states. By 2045, the minority share of the total US population is projected to increase to 46%. According to the Minority 2018 Small Business Trends survey, the number of black-owned small businesses in the United States increased by a staggering 400% in a year-over-year time period from 2017 to 2018. The new survey, which was conducted by Guidant Financial and LendingClub, interviewed more than 2600 business owners and aspiring entrepreneurs. It found that 45% of all small businesses in the country were owned by minority ethnic groups in 2018. This is a dramatic uptick from 2015, when the total percentage of minority business owners was 15%. The largest minority group of respondents was African American at 19%, followed by Hispanic at 14%, Asian at 8%, and Native American at 4%.

These demographic trends will continue to have a significant impact on supplier diversity. First, due to the increased population numbers, the number of minorities and women entering the entrepreneurial arena will likely increase. Thus, it is more likely than not that companies will continue to encounter more diverse suppliers in the future. Companies with strong supplier diversity programs will be better able to identify and develop these young companies into valuable supply relationships. Second, the increased purchasing power of minorities as a customer segment presents the opportunity to market the use of a diverse supplier base. Many multinational companies are already targeting minority segments by focusing on the company's use of minority suppliers.

With the projected increase in population share, minority groups' impact on the US economy is expected to grow as well. By 2045, minority purchasing power may reach $4.3 trillion, compared to $1.3 trillion in 2000. Some estimate go as high as $6.1 trillion if income parity were eliminated by this time, accounting for 44% or as much as 70% of the total increase of purchasing power from 2000 to 2045.

When examining supplier diversity through this lens, it makes perfect business sense for global corporations, mid-sized companies, and the businesses that do business with them to continue cultivating and growing their supplier diversity program efforts and using them to further connect with minority communities. Companies with a diverse supplier base stand to build lasting relationships with these dynamic multicultural markets. *Why?* Because when minority-owned businesses thrive, communities of color and the communities that they represent thrive. Diverse businesses, which are more likely to hire locally and employ people with similar backgrounds, work as powerful forces for economic development. With communities of color slated to become the majority in less than 30 years, how minority-owned businesses fair may determine the sustainability and strength of the entire nation.

CVM Solutions, an international supplier diversity solutions provider and a leading advisor to supplier diversity programs, set out to learn more about the best practices, challenges, frustrations, and triumphs that diverse suppliers deal with every day as they look to grow and become more successful. In 2017, CVM conducted their first comprehensive survey to give diverse businesses an opportunity to share their stories and their experiences. They released a report in 2018 based on participants' answers. According to the report, "Supplier diversity is indeed at a tense crossroads. The political shift in the U.S. in 2017, which included a more pro-business attitude, has diverse suppliers uncertain of their place. Will supplier diversity programs that had increasingly grown over the years begin to pull back? Or will companies continue to pursue diverse suppliers with their previous fervor?" Many responses reflected this uncertainty and frustration. Nevertheless, opportunities remain strong for diverse suppliers, many of whom are seeing their businesses thrive as they partner with companies committed to supplier diversity.

The 380 responses to the CVM survey provided valuable insight into the state of supplier diversity from the diverse suppliers' perspective, including the fact that:

- 92% of minority-owned businesses that responded are certified by an appropriate reporting agency; 87% of women-owned businesses are also certified.
- 62% of respondents have been in business for more than 11 years.
- 21% of diverse suppliers are designated as such by at least ten partner corporations.
- 42% of respondents received at least one opportunity via a diverse supplier registration portal in 2017.
- 82% of respondents are more likely as consumers to buy from corporations with supplier diversity programs, which was about the same as the previous year.
- 74% of respondents said that networking at industry events is one of their top three ways to connect with partners.
- 62% of diverse suppliers actively pursue government contracts (Figs. 4.1, 4.2, 4.3, 4.4, 4.5, 4.6, 4.7, 4.8, 4.9, and 4.10).

The survey asked the participants many questions about their challenges and their successes. The following are some of the respondents' answers.

What Is Your Biggest Challenge in the Supplier Diversity Space?

- "A lot of companies support supplier diversity, but it's more to do with if the diverse supplier is less expensive than a non-diverse supplier. The initiative is there in name."
- "The ability to find the correct individual in the supplier diversity department to actually speak with."
- "All corporations and governments do not consider SBEs to be in the same category as other diverse suppliers. SBEs are not on the same playing field as other diverse vendors. The bias is ridiculously obvious at every turn."
- "Being given a chance to show performance capability when my business has yet to secure an opportunity. How do we gain experience if an opportunity is not presented?"

- "Brand awareness and breaking into new accounts with a stigma that you can only do small or low-level tasks."
- "Competition from certain areas who offer lesser quality, but at a lesser price. At this time, it seems pricing dictates the market, whereas the message of buying quality would be beneficial for product longevity."
- "Too often, supplier diversity people are not integrated into procurement and/or do not have the authority to connect our company with the decision makers who can use our services."
- "Demand for proof that is beyond ridiculous. Not everyone has access to audited financials. This costs too much for a small business. (Sometimes it feels like) the certification process is in place to eliminate and alienate more than actually help."
- "Having corporate customers realize that for a small company to compete for their business, there needs to be an orchestration of partnerships to compete with the larger, well-funded competitors."

Fig. 4.1 Which industry/sector best corresponds to your organization. Source: CVM Solutions, State of Supplier Diversity Report—Diverse Suppliers (2017)

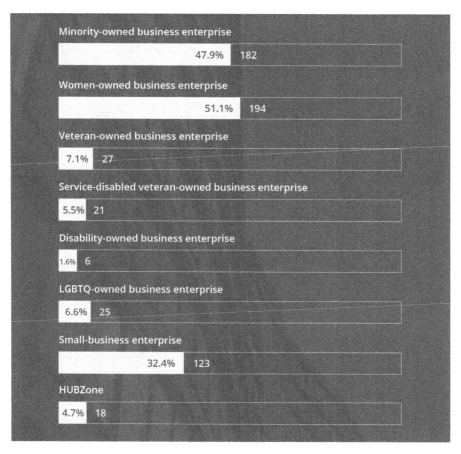

Fig. 4.2 Which category of supplier diversity pertains to your organization? Source: CVM Solutions, State of Supplier Diversity Report—Diverse Suppliers (2017)

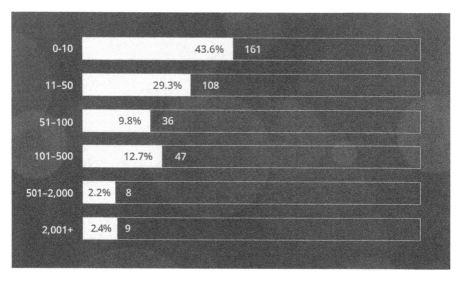

Fig. 4.3 How many employees do you have? Source: CVM Solutions, State of Supplier Diversity Report—Diverse Suppliers (2017)

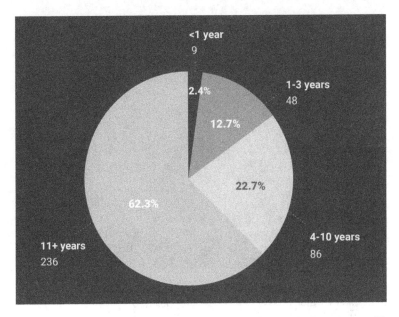

Fig. 4.4 How long have you been in business? Source: CVM Solutions, State of Supplier Diversity Report—Diverse Suppliers (2017)

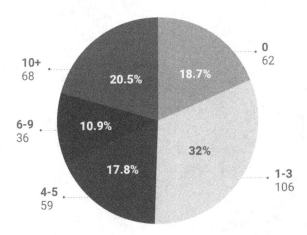

Fig. 4.5 How many corporations is your company working with as a diverse supplier? Source: CVM Solutions, State of Supplier Diversity Report—Diverse Suppliers (2017)

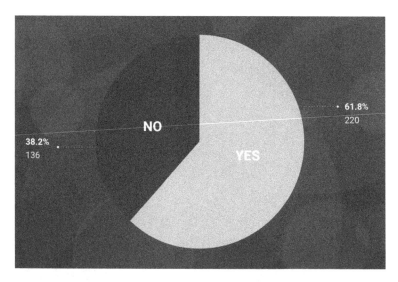

Fig. 4.6 Do you actively pursue government entities as clients? Source: CVM Solutions, State of Supplier Diversity Report—Diverse Suppliers (2017)

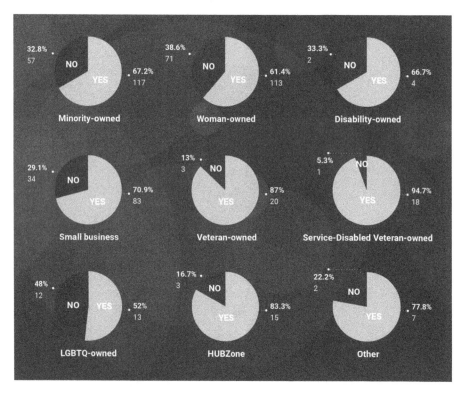

Fig. 4.7 Breakdown by diversity category. Source: CVM Solutions, State of Supplier Diversity Report—Diverse Suppliers (2017)

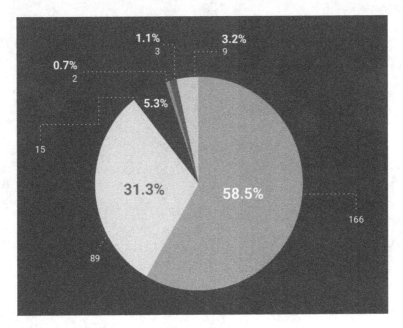

Fig. 4.8 How many opportunities did you receive from supplier diversity registration portals in 2017? Source: CVM Solutions, State of Supplier Diversity Report—Diverse Suppliers (2017)

- "My biggest challenge is convincing corporations that even though my company is small, we will provide exceptional service with superior results if given the opportunity."
- "The stigma of poor quality."
- "Being taken seriously and only being seen as extra spend, not budget spend."

What Do You Enjoy Most About Supplier Diversity Programs?

- "Access to networking opportunities with the organizations I am affiliated with."
- "An equal opportunity to bring our special kind of customer service to customers we normally wouldn't have the chance to partner with."
- "Being able to break down barriers."
- "Meeting global customers' expectations as a small company for over 45 years is an achievement. We are proud of creating a globally known company."
- "Getting a foot in the door and not having to worry about the reaction if they do figure out that I'm gay."

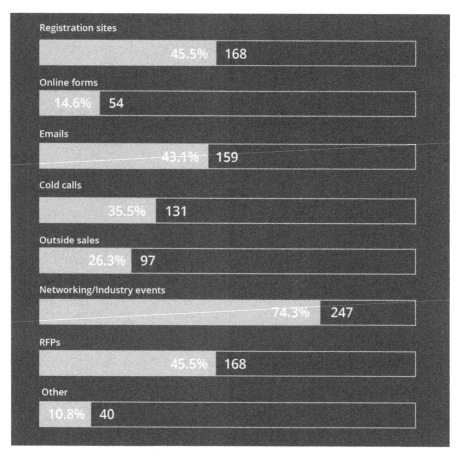

Fig. 4.9 What are your primary ways to find corporations to partner with? Source: CVM Solutions, State of Supplier Diversity Report—Diverse Suppliers (2017)

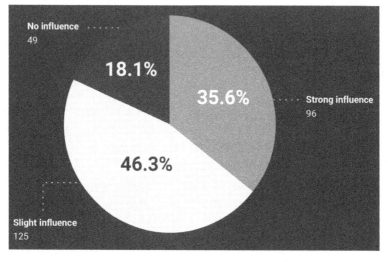

Fig. 4.10 Does an organization with a supplier diversity program influence whether or not you will buy from them as a consumer? Source: CVM Solutions, State of Supplier Diversity Report—Diverse Suppliers (2017)

- "Getting opportunities to bid work we would not have had before."
- "I strongly support women in business and STEM as an advocate. It feels like a good community. We offer innovation and diverse thoughts."
- "It builds a foundation for excellence in the workplace with disparate views, opinions, and expertise."
- "LGBTQ businesses have a seat at the table."
- "The leveling of the playing field for small businesses to win contracts when up against larger competitors with greater resource."

Part III

Designing an Effective Supplier Diversity Program

5

Foundations for a Supplier Diversity Program

Since its inception during the 1970s, the supplier diversity initiative has faced tremendous obstacles in replacing existing practices in the ways companies work with suppliers. Legal challengers have described the changes as "reverse discrimination" or as a violation of the Equal Protection Clause of the Fourteenth Amendment of the US Constitution. Meanwhile, diverse business owners have raced to acquire the elusive "experience" that is often used as an excuse to overlook them. Further, the perceptions of increased risks and decreased quality by using diverse businesses, hidden prejudices, and conscious and unconscious biases have made work for both, supplier diversity practitioners and diverse businesses, an uphill battle. Over time, however, companies have come to realize that supplier diversity and working with suppliers that may resemble their customers offer a more direct return on investment and tangible benefits to the organization through increased market penetration, increased spend with small and diverse vendors, and increased access to diverse markets.

To understand the foundations needed to build a supplier diversity program, we must appreciate how these programs impact the organization and the benefits that can be derived. According to a report commissioned by the National Women's Business Council, the case for supplier diversity continues to evolve from one of social good to one of financial pragmatism. Further, supplier diversity programs also provide a positive benefit for the corporate supply chain in that they can increase efficiency, flexibility, and diversity, while also offering emerging firms important opportunities for sustainable growth.

Another unexpected advantage is the number of intangible benefits that companies that work with diverse suppliers accrue. As conversations about

© The Author(s) 2019
K. K. Porter, *Implementing Supplier Diversity*, https://doi.org/10.1007/978-3-319-94394-7_5

the work-life balance continue to force their way into boardrooms, companies will increasingly look to create a more holistic model for their stakeholders. Senior leaders have come to realize that not all metrics that contribute to the well-being of an organization are quantifiable. In fact, the things that are most important to employees or customers are often not measurable with quantifiable metrics. For organizations that are still not sure about how to communicate the value of incorporating a diverse supplier program into their overall structure and strategy, below is a list of five intangible benefits of having such a program:

1. **Strong Reputation**. An organization's reputation is one of its greatest assets. Talk is cheap and vendors can see through superficial efforts. A supplier diversity program is a practical way for a company to build its reputation as an incubator and supporter of innovation, inclusivity, and diversity. By tying the benefits of supplier diversity to a company's core values and creating messaging to let potential partners and consumers know about a new diverse supplier program, a company can prove that it is walking the walk.
2. **Recognized Leadership**. To become a thought leader in the supplier diversity space both in and out of any given industry, a company should develop best practices with proven results and couple them with a strong corporate reputation. Company leaders should then promote the company's initiatives and further cement its position by publishing white papers and by speaking at conferences.
3. **Successful Partnerships**. Establishing relationships with diverse suppliers and other corporations' supplier diversity program staff can lead to mutually beneficial partnerships. For example, a friendly supplier captured through a company's supplier portal might see a bid opportunity and bring to that company's leadership a cutting-edge solution that volleys it ahead of the competition. Or a supplier diversity manager at a firm might meet with a supplier whose product is not a fit with that company and pass that supplier's information along to another firm that might be able to make use of the supplier. In short, relationships can have wide-ranging, unexpected benefits.
4. **Agility and Adaptability**. Because diverse businesses are usually small and are often aware of the latest trends and processes in their respective industries, they tend to be more agile than their traditional-minded counterparts. Partnering with diverse suppliers gives a company an advantage when it comes to adapting to the marketplace. Imagine having a product that, after a slight modification by consumers, suddenly catches the broader public's interest. To capture that revenue, a company needs to modify its

design or to offer the tools to consumers so they can do so on their own—then it needs to ramp up production quickly. A company needs to determine whether its supply chain can handle an increase in production and whether current suppliers can help it get the modified product to consumers fast.

5. *Compliance*. A company must address compliance issues for no other reason than to stay in the good graces of the federal government. For companies that contract with the federal government, supplier diversity is more than a good business practice—it's mandated in the contract. For a contractor whose contract for goods and services is expected to exceed $700,000 ($1.5 million for construction), the US government requires the company to set and meet aggressive goals of subcontracting spend with underrepresented small businesses from specified categories. Federal contracts can lead to a major boost for a company's bottom line, which is a tangible benefit directly connected to a successful supplier diversity program.

The overlap of organizational benefits and the undeniable positive impact for small businesses makes supplier diversity an impactful and necessary strategy for businesses and organizations alike.

Once a company is sold on the idea of a supplier diversity program, the next step is to establish a foundation for the program. Establishing the foundation is very different from best practices, which identify specific tactics and programming that will be used once the program is up and running. Establishing a foundation entails fostering a certain environment in the company necessary for the launching of a supplier diversity program. Building such a program is a lot like building a house. Before you can even think about getting a builder and reviewing plans, you need to evaluate your finances and maybe even shift financial priorities. Additionally, everyone who is a stakeholder in the house will need to understand and accept the sacrifices that will be required of them so that the investment is a long-term success.

So how does leadership ensure that an organization has the right foundation for a supplier diversity program? A genuine desire to create an inclusive procurement process and to assist the small and diverse business community is a prerequisite. Below are a few additional ways to address organizational culture, commitment from the top, incorporation as part of the strategic planning process, the willingness to take risks, and the identification of key partners. All of these components are essential for creating the foundation for a successful supplier diversity program.

Strong Corporate Culture. Success with supplier diversity starts with organizational culture. An organization that values diversity and makes a commitment to ingrain diversity into its business practices is positioned to succeed with supplier diversity. Companies must first settle the philosophical debate about the value of diversity by engaging in dialogue and providing information and data about population trends to everyone in the organization. Companies should seek to change employee mindsets by challenging beliefs about supplier diversity and creating a climate where procurement professionals are supported and rewarded for diversifying the supply chain. The organizational culture must be one that is enthusiastic about supplier diversity and actively pursues it. That is, it must be a culture in which buyers are encouraged to seek creative ways to partner with minority suppliers, who are then oriented with the buying processes of the firm, encouraged to express their opinions, and allowed to learn from their mistakes.

Accountability and Commitment. Commitment to supplier diversity must start at the executive level in order to fully leverage supplier diversity benefits. A study conducted by the National Minority Supplier Development Council (NMSDC) found that 10 of the 11 top supplier diversity organizations had an active or moderate level of participation from the president and/ or CEO. Leaders must demonstrate their faith in supplier diversity, and procurement professionals must help leadership understand how achieving supplier diversity goals will deliver business results and position the company for growth.

Corporate Alignment. Supplier diversity is successful when it is incorporated into the company's business planning process and clearly communicated, both internally and externally. Executive and line management must align overall corporate goals with supplier diversity goals, including demographic trends, procurement goals, and benefits. This can be accomplished by the following:

- *Tracking expenditures*: Supplier diversity expenditures should be tracked by department or cost center and reviewed with senior management on a regular basis. This will help keep supplier diversity goals on track and identify key areas for attention and future goal setting.
- *Searching for new partners online*: Use of information technology as a dynamic tool for identifying and communicating with diverse suppliers. Any company that is serious about supplier diversity should have a highly visible link on its website that provides information about its program. An internet presence can help a company reach supplier diversity goals if suppliers are able to register and certify online.

- *Using outreach events*: Outreach events, including networking, conferences, and matchmaking, provide opportunities for buyers and suppliers to interface in person. These events enable potential suppliers to get a feel for doing business with a company and serve as excellent forums for information exchange and dialogue. As the supplier diversity lead for the University of Florida, we coordinate the Annual Small Business Opportunity Fair + Summit, which links customers, purchasing representatives, and our first-tier suppliers to the diverse business network.
- *Creating a formal process*: Companies should tie supplier diversity to the main processes of the firm, including long-term strategic planning, evaluation, and even compensation plans. Whatever gets measured usually gets done, and stakeholders perform differently when they have a vested interest and know that their compensation is intimately tied to the success of the program.

Entrepreneurial Spirit. Changing times call for new approaches. Supplier diversity programs should routinely reassess their systems and consider innovative ways to develop and assist minority suppliers to improve and grow. Some non-traditional measures that I have implemented include seeking new sources of funding (i.e., grants); engaging other successful minority businesses as key allies, partners, and mentors; and developing programming to address the specific needs of a particular group, such as women entrepreneurs. Operating programs according to the status quo puts a company at risk of becoming stagnant and never reaching its full potential.

Developing Win-Win Relationships. Creative solutions for supplier diversity may come from joint ventures, strategic alliances, or outsourcing arrangements. One phenomenon that affects many businesses is the proliferation of mergers and acquisitions. Mergers have critically impacted the procurement process by decreasing the number of suppliers but increasing the size and capacity of those who remain, particularly first-tier suppliers. The result is that purchasers are entering into longer-term, exclusive arrangements with a limited number of suppliers. Currently, many minority businesses lack the size, capital, expertise, or infrastructure to compete for these selective supplier positions. Minority suppliers and contracting companies alike must seek out opportunities to partner, collaborate, and form strategic alliances with other firms in order to enter larger markets and gain a competitive edge.

For minority businesses, strategic alliances are tremendously beneficial, whether those partnerships are with other diverse suppliers or with majority-owned firms. Companies will be better able to provide the scale and scope of their services without additional capital requirements and to position themselves to seek equity investment in the future. In addition, national certifying agencies such as NMSDC have now made it possible for minority firms to certify firms, even with a non-minority partner, so long as the minority partner maintains at least 51% ownership in the company. While mergers and acquisitions are not for every firm, evidence suggests that these strategic alliances are vital for success in supplier diversity.

Institute for Supply Management® (ISM®)

The Institute for Supply Management® (ISM®) is the first and largest not-for-profit professional supply management organization worldwide. Founded in 1915, ISM® has over 50,000 members located in 100 countries. In 2011, ISM® introduced the Certified Professional in Supplier Diversity (CPSD) qualification to create experts who could help guide their companies through supplier diversity issues, harness underutilized, innovative suppliers, and tap into new markets. This was not only relevant in that it helped to differentiate experienced supplier diversity practitioners and cultivate the professional status of supplier diversity leaders within organizations. It also helped to further formalize a function that could sometimes be perceived as a cursory add-on function rather than a critical business function.

In 2017, the institute assembled a group of supplier diversity professionals from leading corporations, higher education institutions, and so on to discuss how job titles and roles have changed within the supplier diversity field. This definitively identified the competencies needed for today's supplier diversity professional and outlined those tasks that provide the foundation for an industry standard in developing a world-class supplier diversity program and provided the initial framework for the next iteration of the CPSD exam (Table 5.1).

Table 5.1 Certified professional in supplier diversity exam specification

Competency area	Task
A. Developing business case/obtaining executive support	SD-A-1 Integrate supplier diversity into the organization's mission, vision and commitment statements or the overall business strategy SD-A-2 Consult with and advise senior management on developing and integrating supplier diversity strategies into business practices SD-A-3 Integrate supplier diversity with corporate diversity, supply management and other business initiatives
B. Developing a supplier diversity program	SD-B-1 Develop, implement and integrate short- term and long-term supplier diversity programs and initiatives SD-B-2 Create a company website, database and/or directory of diverse suppliers SD-B-3 Establish annual supplier diversity goals in alignment with supply management and business goals SD-B-4 Develop strategies and procedures for integrating diverse suppliers into supply management and sales enablement processes SD-B-5 Develop and implement supplier diversity best practices and standards SD-B-6 Develop and implement supplier diversity initiatives for prime suppliers
C. Project management for supplier diversity professionals	SD-C-1 Perform project management activities
D. Influencing and partnering with internal stakeholders	SD-D-1 Consult with and advise stakeholders on developing and integrating supplier diversity initiatives into business practices and identifying new opportunities for diverse suppliers SD-D-2 Provide training on diverse supplier sourcing practices (including organizational and government requirements) to internal stakeholders

Copyright 2017, Institute for Supply Management®
Source: Institute for Supply Management® (ISM®) Certified Professional in Supplier Diversity Exam Specification ©2017

6

Best Practices for a Successful Supplier Diversity Program

If you were to ask a group of supplier diversity professionals what makes their program successful, you would likely get very different and possibly conflicting answers, depending on the era they entered the field, their programs' stage of maturity, their industry, their experience, or the culture of their organization. These factors make identifying definitive elements of a successful program arduous, but they also make the search fascinating, as there is no single recipe for success. While some process and policy consistency is required, supplier diversity programs must be adapted to reflect the cultural norms of the organization; the availability and capacity of viable businesses; and the expectations of their customers, leadership, and stakeholders within the community in which the organizations operate.

According to Brian Tippens, the chief diversity officer for Hewlett-Packard and a noted subject-matter expert on global diversity and sustainability, "There is no global supplier diversity "cookie cutter-method" for implementation. It is a mistake for companies to believe they can be successful by simply adopting a "copy exactly" approach and transporting the companies' U.S. supplier diversity tools, processes, and policies into non-U.S. locations. While some process and policy consistency is required, supplier diversity programs must be adapted to reflect the cultural and societal norms of the geographies in which they are implemented."

By the 2000s, after years of investment in programs, corporations were looking for ways to quantify their successes. According to Dr. Fred McKinney—the foremost historian on supplier diversity and former managing director of the minority business programs at the Dartmouth College's Tuck School of Business and former executive director of the New England National Minority Supplier

© The Author(s) 2019
K. K. Porter, *Implementing Supplier Diversity*, https://doi.org/10.1007/978-3-319-94394-7_6

Development Council—Ralph G. Moore & Associates (RGMA) was perhaps the first to develop a commercially viable and valid tool for measuring the quality of corporate supplier development programs during this era. The RGMA scale ranks corporations from "no program" to "world-class program." A consistent theme of the RGMA scale is engagement between the supplier diversity leader and C-level corporate leadership. Once corporate leadership was engaged in supplier diversity and supplier diversity became a key performance indicator, procurement officials were much more likely to use diverse suppliers. RGMA's tool led many corporations to adopt best practices that were also incorporated into the National Minority Supplier Development Council's (NMSDC) best practices. A list of NMSDC's best practices is as follows:

(1) he corporate governance body has established a minority supplier development program as a policy of the corporation.
(2) The CEO has issued a minority supplier development policy that articulates the rationale supporting the initiative. The CEO ensures that this policy is communicated to staff and implemented.
(3) The CEO has appointed appropriate full-time staff and resources for minority supplier development.
(4) There is an executive advisory council/committee composed of key stakeholders to drive the program's progress.
(5) All levels of management are accountable for minority supplier development.
(6) Management directs that supplier diversity be incorporated in the business planning cycle.
(7) Is housed in the procurement department for most companies and business models but should be a part of the organization's umbrella diversity strategy.
(8) There is a written supplier diversity corporate policy that clearly defines executive management commitment and measures success.
(9) Minority business utilization/metrics are included in annual performance goals for the corporation and for each business unit/division of the firm.
(10) A minority supplier development strategy emanates from a business strategy and is not just a "social" policy statement.

Ingrid Watkins: Founder and CEO, IWCG Consulting

Having spent 15 years of my corporate career at The Coca-Cola Company as a supplier diversity lead, I have watched the industry evolve and grow tremendously. In many ways, these changes have been quite positive. Unfortunately, some have been disappointingly counterproductive. In the early years, supplier diversity was a core corporate initiative, mainly because those in leadership roles had vision, passion, and unwavering commitment. Putting aside the academics, processes, procedures, and strategic planning that some may consider imperative elements, the true drivers of successful programs were the old school diversity leaders, people like Greta Davis, former VP of supplier diversity at Time Warner; Johnnie Booker, retired supplier diversity director at The Coca-Cola Company; and Harriet Michel, former president of the NMSDC, a leading diverse business certification and advocacy organization. Harriet Michel once told me, "Supplier diversity leaders must have passion. You cannot sell what you do not believe in." To this day, I still reinforce this mantra with employees in my own consulting agency.

Those trailblazers and thought-leaders possessed pure, unadulterated passion. Their love of their communities, their genuine desire to see them thrive and grow, and the understanding that when a diverse supplier won a corporate contract, there would be a far-reaching economic impact for the community— that was what inspired me to pursue this profession. Those leaders preached that we had to look beyond the transaction itself and consider the trickle-down impact: jobs, college dreams realized, home ownership, savings and investment accounts, retirement funds, and philanthropy within the community. These supplier diversity champions were driven by this knowledge and understanding. They utilized their positions and power to create programs that not only enabled diverse suppliers to gain access to contract opportunities but also provided training and development so they could grow their businesses and be in a better position to compete and win even more bids, sometimes against larger, non-diverse competitors.

In the early 2000s, supplier diversity was a high-priority corporate initiative. The profession was a bustling community of strong leaders on a mission, and there was no compromising. It was a business-critical initiative that was executed effectively and with remarkable results. The measure of the success of a program was not just about spend; that was just one metric. It was also measured by the number of diverse suppliers who won contracts. The success formula for a program looked something like this:

$$\text{Quantity}\left(\#\text{ of diverse suppliers}\right)+\text{spend}=\text{success}$$

When companies used this formula, the diverse supplier pools increased, spend targets were met, and the supplier diversity industry excelled and thrived. It was also during this era that NMSDC was the most powerful it had ever been. It was led by an uncompromising powerhouse, Harriet Michel. Michel understood that the C-suite connection was imperative, and she made those leaders her counterparts, her go-to corporate contacts. I recall hearing many times that there was not a CEO of a major US company that would not take her call. I don't know if that was true, but I do know that it was not uncommon to attend an NMSDC event and see many of those top execs on panels or on the dais as keynote speakers. With that level of visibility and participation, we can only assume that there is some truth to that rumor.

NMSDC played a critical role in ensuring the success of corporate supplier diversity programs. The organization guided the industry and was instrumental in setting the standards and guidelines for supplier diversity program management. They began conducting best practices trainings for supplier diversity leaders, industry group networks that shared information, and high-performing vendors. They also enacted successful policies to ensure that diverse suppliers had opportunities across a number of corporate supply chains. NMSDC had a clearly defined objective: to provide the blueprint for successful programs. The supplier diversity leaders' role was to execute those plans within their organizations.

NMSDC was not the only entity to set best practices. Created in 2001, the Billion Dollar Roundtable (BDR) recognized and celebrated corporations that achieved spending of at least $1 billion with minority and women-owned suppliers. BDR serviced a small but elite group of best-in-class corporations and promoted supply chain diversity excellence through the production of white papers and trainings. BDR further defined measures of success and made recommendations to corporations that aspired to join.

There was a perceived correlation between a corporation's commitment to diverse business communities and the effort and resources it put into its supplier diversity program. If the corporation had a robust program, the perception was that it was serious about doing business with minorities. If it did not put forth much effort in building a program, it sent a different message, which was not always positive. Studies on consumer behavior show that diverse consumers tend to be extremely brand loyal. Companies began to pay attention to this correlation. They recognized the measurable benefits of their engagements with these communities and the marketable value in promoting this initiative as a cornerstone of a corporation's culture.

It should be noted that a successful program is not built overnight. It often takes more than a few years for a program to take off. Creating an effective program requires a strategic plan, cross-functional effort, and a long-term commitment to the implementation of the right systems, protocols, and policies. As a former senior executive in a leading global company that was routinely recognized for its supplier diversity efforts and a practitioner with colleagues in a number of industries, from almost every *Fortune* 500 company with a supplier diversity program or initiative, I have found that the common components in the most successful supplier diversity programs include executive leadership support, a dedicated team, a viable budget, the ability to impact policy, and access to technology.

Executive leadership support. In the early days of supplier diversity, starting a new program meant challenging the status quo, the corporate culture. Proponents of such programs were suggesting a different way of doing things, and not all stakeholders were eager to embrace the revolution. To facilitate this culture change and to move toward more diverse and inclusive business practices, supplier diversity relied on executive leadership support to communicate the business case, the policy, and the strategic plan to the organization. Although supplier diversity created the policies, facilitated the change management, and coordinated the trainings, the directive to initiate the change had to be pushed out and down from the C-suites. The initiative was communicated as a business-critical company initiative, not just as something a small supplier diversity team was driving. Early corporate efforts usually failed because of the lack of a top-down commitment, and the same is still true today.

Dedicated team. At Coca-Cola, I was fortunate to work in an environment where we had a dedicated team accountable for managing all of the various aspects of the program. The department consisted of a director or VP and a team of three staff members. Our VP set policies and procedures, and managed relationships with internal and external stakeholders, including company executives. She was also responsible for ensuring a regular meeting cadence with company leadership to report progress and milestones and to ensure that supplier diversity was aligned with and included in the company's strategic planning. The team routinely collaborated with procurement and other departments to identify opportunities for diverse suppliers and secure stakeholder buy-in and support from the organization.

Budget. An effective program requires an adequate budget. Managers act as relationship builders. They participate in outreach, serve as brand ambassadors, and engage numerous external stakeholders. One of the secrets of a program's success is robust outreach to external diverse advocacy organizations. As part of the supplier diversity team, I represented Coca-Cola on numerous councils that certify minority and women business enterprises and promote MWBE success including the:

- National Minority Supplier Development Council (NMSDC)
- Women's Business Enterprise National Council (WBENC)
- National LGBT Chamber of Commerce (NGLCC)
- National Veteran Business Development Council (NVBDC)
- United States Hispanic Chamber of Commerce (USHCC)
- National Black Chamber of Commerce (NBCC)
- US Pan Asian American Chamber of Commerce (USPAACC)

To engage these organizations, we paid membership dues, sponsorships, and/or conference fees. While this represented a significant part of our budget, it was a necessary component of our outreach efforts as it was a cost-effective way to source and vet multiple suppliers for upcoming contract opportunities, allowed us to connect and network with diverse suppliers, and enabled face time with suppliers who we may not otherwise have had the opportunity to meet. Some of the most impressive suppliers I have encountered and introduced to the Coca-Cola supply chain were those I met at these outreach events. For multinational corporations such as Coca-Cola, it became less efficient to have new vendors meet with us at the office or conduct onsite introductory meetings. External relationship management, outreach, and supplier engagement became critical elements of our program's success.

Ability to impact policy. Corporate programs cannot thrive without a strategic sustainability plan, and supplier diversity is no different. Leading supplier diversity programs usually outline a three-to-five-year plan that defines metrics and details how the program will continue to grow versus the previous year. This plan usually details upcoming procurement opportunities to be initiated by the organization and includes a strategic diverse supplier strategic sourcing plan which identified the types of vendors needed to support these opportunities and whether they were already in the organizational supply chain or would need to be brought in. We needed to develop a proactive rather than reactive approach which required us to create a collaborative relationship with our procurement department. In my experience, if supplier diversity is not included in the initial planning stages of the contract opportunity, organizations risk being too late to adequately source diverse suppliers as well as allow sufficient time for potential diverse suppliers to mobilize and respond to opportunities.

Access to technology. The supplier diversity team is responsible for building the business case, managing change, implementing technology tools and processes, and coordinating trainings. The ability to identify, extract, and compile spend reports with diverse suppliers requires integration with the corporation's accounting system. The role of spend reporting is delegated to a member of the supplier diversity team who has skills and abilities in accounting or data management, and some departments are fortunate enough to have a dedicated spend analyst. Direct spend reports are extracted from the company's payables system, but second-tier reports are reported in from prime suppliers through a manual Tier II-spend process or technology portal. Years ago, the preferred supplier diversity tool providers were AECsoft and CVM. Both companies were minority-owned, which enabled supplier diversity to count these technology tools as diversity expenditure. These companies experienced fast growth and offered invaluable automation to supplier diversity processes, which improved efficiency and productivity. Both companies were eventually sold to majority companies, enabling new, diverse-owned technology companies to enter the market. These new entrants include B2Gnow, ConnXus, VIVA, Supplier Gateway, and Diversity Reporting Solutions (DRS). All of these companies provide tools to create a variety of diversity spend data reports and dashboards, as well as other technology services.

Collaborating with Internal Stakeholders

Traditionally, supplier diversity involved partnering more with regional buyers and business unit leads to act as company representatives at regional advocacy organization outreach events. If a company takes this path and implements this practice, supplier diversity should ensure that these fill-in extensions are well versed on supplier diversity's objectives, and they should come prepared to speak intelligently on upcoming procurement opportunities and on the requirements for participating in the RFP (request for proposal) process. An RFP is a detailed specification used to procure complex goods and services and is frequently used by procurement organizations. There is nothing more discouraging to a minority business than to travel to a conference and wait in long lines only to arrive at a corporate vendor's booth and encounter someone who is uninformed, disinterested, or just pulling a shift. Such a connection does not benefit the minority business enterprise (MBE) and can create a negative perception of a brand's commitment.

Although much has changed over the years, some things have stayed the same: Corporate policy and C-suite engagement remain essential to a successful supplier diversity program. An effective and sustainable supplier diversity program must engage, obtain support from, and align with C-suite executives. A robust program requires a senior leader who has co-ownership of the program and who is fully invested in its success. When organizational changes are underway, an effective supplier diversity leader ensures the adoption of a strong corporate policy and prepares a compelling business case that links supplier diversity to the company's revenue generation.

Measuring Success

Let's face it, measuring success in any organization can be difficult because success is often a moving target. So then how does a company measure success in supplier diversity? It is important to start by acknowledging that diversity is not a destination so much as a long-lasting journey. A company can certainly measure the number of contracts, the total spend to diverse vendors, and all of the other quantifiable metrics readily identifiable. But my years as a consultant and my career in supplier diversity at one of the most recognizable brands in the world—and one of the leaders in supplier diversity—have changed the way I think about success. I have realized that the number of diverse firms added to the supply chain is rarely used as a measure of success because more major corporations are meeting their targets with fewer suppliers. This practice has been controversial, especially given that advocates have made the economic impact of supplier diversity the centerpiece of their argument for the business case. There are those who argue that contracting with a few large suppliers can have just as much impact on the diverse community as multiple supplier contracts, but another school of thought holds that the number of diverse firms in the supply chain is the most impactful measure of success because it enables larger numbers of diverse suppliers to receive a piece of the revenue pie.

It would be nice to think that a company that makes supplier diversity a high priority today will also make it a high priority tomorrow, but the truth is, there is considerable turnover in the C-suites of most companies, and the new executives do not always share the same values and priorities as their predecessors. Thus, supplier diversity professionals must constantly reinvent their programs so that they align with the new leaders' planned goals and objectives. The first step is to communicate a compelling business case, which links supplier diversity work to revenue generation, customer retention, and innovation. A pitch might look something like this:

- Multicultural consumers make up a large percentage of our customer base, and our supplier base should reflect our customer base.
- Diverse communities expect our brand to demonstrate inclusive business practices. There could be marketplace backlash if we do not embrace diversity and inclusion and engage diverse suppliers for contract opportunities.

- Supplier diversity provides a competitive advantage when vying for bids, including some federal contracts, university systems, airport authorities and municipalities, and major corporations. Our competitors have strong programs and so should we.
- Our major customers require us to engage diverse suppliers and report spend with these entities on a quarterly basis.

Set Targets and Make Stakeholders Accountable for Meeting Those Targets

Supplier diversity drives the process, but procurement and the business units are the final decision makers. They are ultimately responsible for executing the plan that supplier diversity creates. This being the case, I recommend taking the following steps when it comes time to set targets:

1. Analyze diversity spend for each procurement category and identify opportunities to grow spend with those diverse suppliers currently providing goods and services. That can be done by increasing their scope of work or expanding their offering to additional categories.
2. Ensure that diverse suppliers are included in all RFPs, and when all things are equal, select the diverse supplier.
3. Implement a "limited competition" process. This is accomplished by identifying categories with a high concentration of viable diverse firms (e.g., printing, trucking, and janitorial) and selecting from a pool of diverse firms to compete for the contract.
4. Second-tier spend can help a company meet targets and maximize spend. Encourage your large suppliers to start their own supplier diversity initiatives and report that spend quarterly. That spend can be included in total diversity spend reports and counts toward targets.

Supplier Diversity from Program to Strategy

While a supplier diversity program is essential for a company competing in today's global economy, the most successful organizations are those that have made the transition from program to strategy. These organizations use supplier diversity as a strategic asset that is aligned with the corporate vision, is a contributor to global growth, and is a competitive advantage in a highly diverse economy.

7

Common Mistakes in Design and Implementation

A study by the research firm The Hackett Group, a global leader in business advisory, business benchmarking, and business transformation consulting services, indicates that many companies make several common errors in managing their supplier diversity initiatives. To start, too few companies focus on developing programs that further their corporate goals. Instead, they focus on hitting certain numbers or gaining recognition from their customers or from other companies within their industries. These are certainly not bad aspirational goals, but they may not provide all the value that a more comprehensive approach might deliver. And even when programs align with corporate objectives, management often fails to ensure alignment at the operational level.

Hackett's study also found that most programs rely on overly simplistic measures to evaluate their programs. For instance, about 90% of organizations track their percentage of spending with diverse suppliers. However, fewer than half of the study participants track the percentage of diverse suppliers in the total pool of suppliers. Moreover, only 10% analyze the impact of their supplier diversity efforts on revenue or market share.

Another common mistake is failing to align program objectives with the number of diverse suppliers with whom an organization works. This is key because this figure varies with a business' goals. For instance, B2B organizations often are best served by focusing on meeting a limited number of larger contracts so they can satisfy government regulations. Consumer-oriented companies, by contrast, may be better served by developing a larger group of suppliers and, thus, raising their market profile.

© The Author(s) 2019
K. K. Porter, *Implementing Supplier Diversity*, https://doi.org/10.1007/978-3-319-94394-7_7

K.T. Harrington: Sales and Marketing Director, B2Gnow

As the sales and marketing director of a leading diversity management software company managing over half a trillion dollars in contracts for compliance, I speak with existing clients and potential clients every day. These clients include airports, transit agencies, ports, Department of Transportation offices, states, cities, counties, housing authorities, and contractors. The one thing that I hear more often than I would like is that as organizational priorities shift, so too does supplier diversity. Too many organizations feel that supplier diversity has shifted from a business imperative to an optional program. In this transition, the "lifts and shifts" look like downsizing and reorganizing.

Teams that had been housed in procurement are moved around to various corporate departments, including human resources (HR), diversity and inclusion (D&I), public relations, and community relations. It is a mistake to view supplier diversity solely as a community relations initiative or a philanthropic program. It does not encompass workforce and does not belong in human resources or diversity and inclusion. It is not a public relations endeavor and does not fit with communications, public relations, or community relations. Supplier diversity is a key procurement initiative, which means that it should be a part of the procurement process. The supplier diversity team should have a seat at the procurement decision-making table and should be a part of supplier sourcing, evaluation, and selection. When supplier diversity is part of procurement, the team can better understand the RFP requirements and can focus on strategic sourcing to ensure that viable and competitive diverse suppliers are included in the process. A supplier diversity lead advocates for the use of diverse suppliers and sets guidelines for inclusive practices. For example, an inclusive corporate policy would ensure that a diverse supplier is included in all RFPs and contracting opportunities. A supplier diversity team positioned outside of procurement is a supplier diversity team that is not functioning as a part of a collaborative procurement model.

There is no question that the early supplier diversity initiatives had a significant impact on the diverse business communities. The industry had clearly defined objectives, passionate leadership, and C-suite support. Many industry observers believe that supplier diversity has lost its prominence within many corporations and that it is not the corporate influencer that it once was. As experienced teams are disbanded, budgets are cut, and C-suite engagement ebbs, it appears that the industry has suffered some damaging blows.

Understanding that the supplier diversity industry has changed and that it is not the corporate priority that it was in the past, leaders who are tasked with coming up with innovative new approaches to achieving their goals must be passionate and committed. Diversity advocacy organizations have renewed their focus on supplier development and outreach activity to foster corporate-to-MBE connectivity and relationship building.

Supplier diversity departments are often hit hardest during corporate downsizing and restructuring, during which teams are reduced in size or eliminated altogether. But as Johnnie Booker, former Global Director of Supplier Diversity for The Coca-Cola Company and president and CEO of The Johnnie Booker Group, argues, "A leader fights for her team to ensure their job security during restructuring. Cost savings can be achieved by cutting non-critical budget items; staff cuts should be the last resort," she adds. Like Booker, I do not subscribe to the notion of doing more with less. When you must perform the same work with fewer resources, the quality of the work invariably suffers. Having experienced leaders at the helm can certainly help, though. Redefining the work, prioritizing, and enlisting support from other departments in the organization can address some resource gaps, particularly in outreach and data reporting.

Recruiting versus *"lift and shift."* Most supplier diversity practitioners agree that companies often make a crucial mistake when a leadership position opens up in a supplier diversity program: they do not attempt to recruit an experienced replacement. Oftentimes companies take the easy route and "lift and shift" managers from another department in the company. This practice is not likely to yield the passion, commitment, and experience needed to start or manage an effective program. Lifting and shifting unqualified and passionless replacements from other departments not only endangers any progress the program made in the past, but also it can stifle future growth. Companies should seriously consider a focused recruitment strategy to ensure that they identify the best qualified applicants, those who will maintain the program and continue its commitment to success.

Resource sharing. Dedicated data analyst roles for diversity spend have been hardest hit by the downsizing trend. To replace those positions, supplier diversity leaders are turning to other departments like accounting and analytics to manage data reporting and analysis. People from these departments may have the ability to extract and report spend, but the responsibility of development strategies for increasing diversity spend by category still requires supplier diversity experience.

Double duty. The dedicated supplier diversity position often becomes a dual role, and managers are required to perform procurement, community relations, and D&I roles in addition to their supplier diversity duties.

When an organization conducts an annual review of its processes and procedures, it should also review the organization's supply chain management programs. Today's real thought leaders are companies that actively mentor, partner with and engage their diverse prime and second-tier suppliers, setting the pace for the future of supplier diversity. Is your organization keeping up with industry's best practices for supplier diversity? How can you tell if your supplier diversity program needs work? Here are four warning signs that your program might have veered off track:

- You expect (and accept) lower standards of quality, accuracy, and timeliness from minority- or women-owned businesses than from other suppliers.
- You periodically scrub your vendor data to make sure your diversity numbers look acceptable, without launching any new supplier diversity initiatives.
- You monitor your prime (Tier I) suppliers but have not implemented a supplier diversity program for your Tier II through Tier IV suppliers or firms that subcontract with your prime.
- You have no effective processes in place to include diverse and unique perspectives in your company's supply chain decisions.

Part IV

Helping Entrepreneurs Use Supplier Diversity Programs to Scale

8

Certifications and Other Tactics to Help Small Firms Leverage, Differentiate, and Win!

Small businesses, especially minority-owned small businesses, are well placed to lead the United States in economic growth in the coming years. The combination of a growing minority population and the number of government-sponsored small business assistance programs makes this a great time to be a minority-owned small business. In fact, companies can do quite well for themselves if they are poised to take advantage of the increased spending power of minority communities and the prevalence of supplier diversity programs.

As of 2007, there were around six million minority-owned firms in the United States. The truth is that the minority population is large, both in terms of size and business influence. Supplier diversity programs and the accompanying government programs designed to assist disadvantaged businesses represent a strategic business opportunity for minority-owned businesses. Getting certified in one or more of these programs is the first step, but following through by delivering great value is what keeps your business in the game in the long term.

Here are some eye-opening facts about minority-owned firms:

- Women-owned businesses generate $1.4 trillion in annual revenue.
- Veteran-owned businesses generate $1.2 trillion in annual sales. They also employ 5.8 million people and have an annual payroll of $210 billion.
- Minorities own 15.1% of all US businesses, which is more than three million firms.
- Approximately 99% of all minority-owned firms are small businesses.

© The Author(s) 2019
K. K. Porter, *Implementing Supplier Diversity*, https://doi.org/10.1007/978-3-319-94394-7_8

The latest reports show that there are more than 12,500 WBENC-certified women-owned businesses, more than 5000 US Business Leadership Network (USBLN)-certified disability-owned businesses, 771 NGLCC-certified LGBTQ-owned businesses, and 11,978 NMSDC-certified Asian-, black-, Hispanic-, and Native American-owned businesses. Minority populations continue to grow faster than the rest of the population, which means that the US population is steadily becoming more diverse. According to the US Department of Labor, over the past ten years, minority-owned businesses have grown at approximately double the rate of all firms in the United States.

Rafael Marrero: CEO, Rafael Marrero & Company

As a former vice president of corporate vendor management, contracts, supply chain, and procurement for MasTec Network Solutions, a division of MasTec (NYSE: MTZ), a $5.1 billion firm, I was responsible for sourcing, vetting, and managing more than 700 subcontractors and suppliers nationwide, representing $1.5 billion in projects on behalf of AT&T, Verizon Wireless, T-Mobile, and Sprint. Although this sounds like a significant number—and we were definitely hitting our participation spend goals—we were only scratching the surface of what could be achieved. According to most industry professionals and supplier diversity practitioners, their biggest issue remains finding qualified vendors. I knew that I could have a significant impact coaching firms to position themselves to take advantage of these opportunities, so in 2002, I started my own firm, Rafael Marrero & Company. As CEO of a government services company and a Hispanic business enterprise (HBE), I have had the opportunity to work on all sides of the industry: as a procurement officer, a consultant, and a contractor. Since starting my firm, we have assisted thousands of minority-, veteran-, and women-owned businesses; HUBZone businesses; and small businesses break into the federal marketplace through Small Business Administration (SBA), minority and small business certifications. One example of a client who experienced explosive growth in a relatively short period of time is Florida-based engineering contractor Miguel Lopez Jr. Inc. Established in Miami, Florida, in 1989, the firm is a second-generation Hispanic family owned and operated construction business specializing in asphalt maintenance, engineering, and site work. The firm's principals are two brothers of Cuban descent: Miguel Lopez and Eduardo Lopez. Both have great customer relationships in their industry, have relevant professional experience, and are hardworking individuals.

After the Great Recession of 2008, the firm's bonding company went out of business and the firm was denied bonding multiple times. This was a major impediment to their development and stunted the firm's growth. The firm had been looking to expand its client base and trying to get into federal government contracting, particularly the SBA 8(a) Business Development Program, which is an extensive business development program that allows the government to set aside and award smaller projects specifically to companies with this designation. They had previously applied for the program twice and gave up due to the daunting amount of paperwork involved. However, Miguel never gave up this hope as he knew the federal government appeared "recession proof" customer. He decided to try a different approach and conducted market research to find a consultant that could assist them in this effort. Ultimately, he retained our services to help his firm break into the federal space.

Through our extensive experience and network with the Small Business Administration (SBA), we first began with tackling their 8(a) application, which was prepared, submitted, and approved by the government within 90 days, which is almost unheard of. Next, we worked on getting the company "procurement and contract ready" in order to create a lasting first impression with US federal government agencies and their buyers. "Contract ready" is a term used by contracting officials to indicate a firm is ready, willing, and able to respond and successfully deliver if a contract is awarded to them. To this effect, we then developed professional marketing materials specific to the federal marketplace. This included the design and creation of a capability statement, a capability briefing presentation, and tweaking the firm's website to include government specific materials and references.

Once we had the necessary marketing materials, we then began to study the firm's top five government agencies and prospects and targeted them via email, phone calls, and personal visits. We attended several industry events in an effort to introduce the firm, establish a presence, and build relationships with the government buyers of his firm's services. It was during this process that we identified several opportunities of interest to the firm. In all, we submitted seven bids in less than six months with five major federal agencies.

We were also able to get him enrolled in the Department of Transportation–sponsored Bonding Program. Participation in the US Department of Transportation's bonding training and coaching series helped Miguel Lopez Jr. Inc. overcome one of its major hurdles for growth: limited bonding. The firm's previous bonding capacity grew exponentially from $1.5 million per project to $10 million per project. The firm's aggregate binding capacity also grew from $4 million to $25 million. This opened the door for the client to receive larger project awards from companies such as Hawkins Construction.

Before working with us, the average construction project previously awarded did not exceed $1.5 million. In 2017, the firm was awarded its single largest construction contract worth $9.2 million.

Since its time with us, Miguel Lopez Jr. Inc. has experienced exponential and sustained growth. In 2015, the firm's gross revenues were $7.5 million. In less than two years, the firm's revenues grew to $17 million. According to the firm's principal and CEO, their firm has grown more in the last two years than in their previous 28 years of existence. It was at this time that they also achieved another significant milestone as they were recognized as one of America's fastest-growing privately owned firms by *Inc.* magazine, growing by more than 140% in less than three years.

Miguel Lopez Jr. Inc. has also seen a substantial increase in employee head-count, having grown from 29 employees in 2015 to 63 employees in 2017. Additionally, due to the increase in business and revenues, we were able to help them secure an SBA 7(a) loan to make yet another one of its dreams come true—moving into a new, state-of-the-art corporate facility in Pembroke Pines, FL!

From the US government's standpoint, supplier diversity is imperative. The federal government has instituted programs to ensure that minority-, veteran-, and women-owned businesses and other disadvantaged small businesses face a more level playing field when competing against bigger suppliers. Without supplier diversity programs, small businesses, especially those owned by minorities, veterans, and women, would face a seemingly insurmountable hurdle when competing against larger corporations.

Achieving small or minority-owned business certification can unlock a firm's potential as a diverse supplier and open up doors to exciting—and growing—public and private sector business programs. At present, there are more than $80 billion in opportunities earmarked for certified small businesses from just four of the agencies that we regularly work with. They anticipate spending approximately $34 billion on goods and services from certified minority-owned and small businesses.

As a supplier diversity professional and a consultant, I believe that it is imperative that we are able to articulate the strategic value and advantages of becoming certified as minority-, veteran-, or women-owned small business. Through my experience as a contracting officer and now as a consultant and a Hispanic business enterprise (HBE), I have come up with what I call *The 10 Currencies Minorities and Small Businesses Get from Becoming a Certified Minority-Owned Business or Diverse Supplier.* Whether contracting with public agencies or private corporations, diverse business professionals should be able to focus on one or more of these "currencies" to encourage a business to get certified:

Inclusion. Accredited minority-, veteran-, and women-owned small businesses can compete for opportunities and RFPs for which they might not have been considered. These new credentials open up a world of corporate and government opportunities to which, as a boutique or a small company, they would not otherwise be exposed. Major corporations develop supplier diversity and inclusion programs with the sole intent of doing business with certified companies. Some are even legally mandated to have a small business subcontracting plan, especially those that are Tier I suppliers themselves. After becoming an MBE, many of our firm's small business clients have been able to win contracts in the construction industry, management consulting, and information and communications technology (ICT) sectors for which they would not have otherwise dreamed of competing.

Resources and choices. There are multiple, private-publicly funded initiatives and programs that provide a vast array of technical assistance to small businesses and aspiring small, women, and veteran entrepreneurs. Among these, the Small Business Administration (SBA) has more than 900 Small Business Development Centers (SBDCs) or service sites across the United States to support business growth and to enhance the creation of new small businesses. These centers serve all populations, including minorities; women; military reservists, active duty personnel, disabled veterans, and those returning from deployment; youth and encore entrepreneurs; and individuals in low- and moderate-income urban and rural areas.

Vetting and credibility. The SBA 8(a) Business Development Program is designed to help level the playing field for qualified participants in this unique, nine-year business development program. This program requires that its minority and small business applicants undergo extensive vetting by US government agencies, including the Office of the Inspector General (OIG). Ethnicity, gender, or previous military service alone does not guarantee program admission. As part of the overall approval and extensive documentation process, applicants must clearly demonstrate that they meet all program requirements to become part of this elite program, which has approximately 7500 participating firms.

Relationships that give you energy or power. Becoming a certified minority-owned business provides small business owners with a new network and community of people who want these businesses to succeed. Doors will open to other small businesses, large corporations, and employee resource groups. Networking opportunities provide opportunities for building relationships with corporate buyers.

Reputation and brand. Here's an interesting fact: Women entrepreneurs are shaping the future of the American economy by employing 7.9 million

American workers. And here's another fact: Veteran-owned businesses generate $1.2 trillion in annual sales, employ 5.8 million people, and have an annual payroll of $210 billion. Besides being great for our economy and for the people of the United States, these impressive statistics act as marketing tools for these businesses and help create a potent brand.

Shared Success. Most government entities at the federal, state, and local levels mandate that a certain percentage of business must go to small and minority-, veteran-, and women-owned businesses. Access to and eligibility for government contracts is a huge benefit of certification for small and minority-owned businesses. It is important to note that firms must still be qualified, but certification is a competitive advantage that changes the game.

"Face time" with key decision makers, stakeholders, and influencers. Many *Fortune* 500 companies have well-developed minority contracting programs. By earning minority or small business federal certification, businesses are almost certainly going to be placed directly in front of decision makers at very large corporations or at government agencies that are committed to doing business with bona fide minority-owned businesses.

Knowledge and legacy. As businesses get certified and accredited as diverse suppliers in the federal supply chain, businesses now have access to customized executive education and business development programs. This may include Ivy League training and technical assistance from prestigious executive education programs such as Northwestern University's Kellogg Advanced Management Education Scholarship Program or Dartmouth College's Tuck College of Business Executive Education Minority Business Entrepreneur Development programs. These celebrated programs provide leadership tools specifically for CEOs of minority-owned firms.

Market intelligence. After completing the minority certification process, businesses are granted access to the large databases used by major corporations, other minority-owned firms, and government entities that support supplier diversity. These databases allow minority businesses to search for prospective customers and clients who will benefit from the product or service provided. Additionally, the company's information will also be featured in these databases so that purchasers can connect with diverse vendors for a particular product or service.

Funding sources and access to capital markets. Becoming certified can also help a company apply for and secure loans through third-party intermediaries such as the Women's Business Development Center or the Small Business Development Center. These organizations will assist in the preparation and submission of loan applications to the SBA, which can be a critical source of capital to get a business up and running. Established small businesses can also obtain such loans in order to acquire additional equipment, expand their employee base, or open another location.

While not every firm experiences the spectacular results, the capital benefits of certification for diverse firms can be immense and can certainly put a firm on the fast track for growth and long term sustainability. It is worth noting that certification also provides a more accurate baseline for tracking and assists diversity professionals in capturing data and reporting on the successes of diverse firms.

9

Community Engagement: Partnerships and M.O.D.E. (Mentorship, Outreach, Development, and Education)

The Chartered Institute of Procurement & Supply defines supplier development as "the process of working with certain suppliers on a one-to-one basis to improve their performance and expand capabilities for the benefit of the buying organization." Supplier development can come in many different forms, from informal initiatives to a formally structured program. There are numerous examples, use cases, and best practices that demonstrate a broad spectrum of supplier development initiatives to fit any size organization or supplier diversity program.

According to CVM Solutions, corporate supplier diversity programs must go above and beyond spend metrics, but in an era of continuous improvement, supplier diversity programs—like most business units within an organization—must figure out how to evolve to remain a resource for the businesses they are servicing. Most do this by driving an even more robust program to promote economic growth through supplier development.

Most mature supplier diversity programs have incorporated some type of supplier development activities within their organizations. As supplier diversity and procurement professionals interact with diverse suppliers, they are often mentoring and offering advice on development. They can also provide other resources that can help the diverse suppliers learn the environment in which they are doing business. The goal of supplier development is to help diverse suppliers become more sustainable in service to the organizations with which they are working and to the marketplace as a whole. Even if a supplier is not currently working with an organization, supplier development can create future value for the organization.

© The Author(s) 2019
K. K. Porter, *Implementing Supplier Diversity*, https://doi.org/10.1007/978-3-319-94394-7_9

Most supplier diversity professionals can offer many success stories that show the importance of investing in supplier development. By focusing on such development, organizations are able to generate many mutually beneficial opportunities, including the following:

- Expanding the competitive landscape (e.g., pricing, service levels and offerings) for the organization's existing vendors and for potential vendors
- Promoting innovation and out-of-the-box thought leadership through the entrance of new products, services, and solutions into a business
- Growing the sources and channels from which to procure products and services
- Showcasing the organization's commitment to the economic growth of the communities in which they operate
- Driving job creation
- Building the capacity of diverse businesses not only to serve the organization more effectively but also to increase their sustainability in the marketplace
- Increasing the organization's customer satisfaction, be it B2B or B2C

Supplier development also affords corporations an opportunity to bring together teams of suppliers to work jointly for the benefit of the company, improving the bottom line in the long run. Additionally, these approaches can showcase the organization's commitment to the economic growth of local communities while also building the capacity of diverse businesses to serve the organization more effectively.

Introducing M.O.D.E.

Ultimately, supplier development as a component of a supplier diversity program is an indicator that the program is vigorous. By working intimately with diverse businesses and building a relationship that extends beyond a single contract or transaction, an organization can become invested in the long-term success of the diverse business, whether they continue to do business with your organization or leverage the relationship to do business with other organizations. In actuality, this is a good thing as it allows the diverse business to build capacity and expand and diversify their customer base.

In addition to advocacy, I have always made supplier development a critical component of any program that I have built and managed and is an area in which I attribute much of the success of my programs. In many ways, I consider the services offered by supplier diversity programs comparable to those offered by other entrepreneurial development organizations, incubators or agencies such as SBDC and SBA, with whom I also frequently collaborate. Serving as an adjunct business instructor has been an enjoyable aspect of my career and has provided me experience in curriculum development, which has been helpful in developing educational programs for entrepreneurs whether for construction firms, professional services firms, or consumer products (goods) firms seeking to establish a business-to-business relationship or other businesses just looking to build their business acumen. This is also an area about which I am frequently asked to speak at conferences and receive regular inquiries about supplier development from my colleagues. When you give businesses the skills they need to succeed, you have secured the viability and sustainability of those businesses for, ideally, a long time to come.

Over the years, I have tweaked my supplier development program strategy to address the needs of the community and the resources available to my program, but it has consistently included some form of what I call "MODE":

M—Mentorship
O—Outreach
D—Development
E—Education

Mentorship. Mentor-protégé programs are designed to encourage large businesses to provide mutually beneficial developmental assistance to small and emerging businesses. Help usually comes in the form of assistance with performance on contracts and subcontracts, the establishment of long-term business relationships and strategic alliances, and the promotion and strengthening of subcontracting opportunities. When used correctly, this is a highly effective programming tool, one that I use consistently. I have seen many businesses gain invaluable experience with assistance from their mentors. By entering into such relationships, protégés position themselves to receive progressively higher-value contracts, annual contracts, and subcontracting opportunities, and they also form strategic alliances that are often a boon to their businesses.

After protégés graduate from the mentor-protégé program, I like to invite them to become mentors so they can provide a firsthand account of their own experiences to a new class of protégés. This is also a means of introducing diversity into the mentor pool, which I consider an important strategy for bringing new firms into the program.

Outreach. In any market, supplier diversity networking and matchmaking events are ubiquitous. They are one of the primary means for small and diverse businesses to connect with their desired customers or clients. We often hold targeted "Meet the Buyers" and "Meet the Primes" events, but I also tend to get creative in this area. Some years ago, I introduced a "Small Business Bus Tour" for the protégés in our mentor-protégé program. We visited several University of Florida project sites in a luxury bus. Participants had a rare opportunity to tour the site, to speak directly with the project's construction manager, and to hear about active and upcoming opportunities. The event was highly successful, and people in the supplier diversity community tell me that it is one of the most anticipated events of the year.

Development. This area focuses on providing opportunities for businesses to build capacity while competing with other firms of comparable size and capability. While contracts designated and exclusive to a specific group, also known as "set-asides," are frowned upon outside of the federal government, development efforts could include targeted small contract programs, preparation for upcoming contract opportunities, continuing services programs or policies that allow preferential points for being or utilizing local or diverse businesses.

Education. Continuing education opportunities vary from organization to organization. Many programs offer workshops that focus on basic business topics such as marketing, social media, finance, access to capital, and bonding. As programs grow and evolve, workshop offerings become more targeted. "Doing Business" workshops are ideal for more mature programs, and so are workshops that focus on a specific area on campus (e.g., athletics, hospitals, catering, bookstores, construction, or professional services). Workshops can also be a great opportunity for strengthening partnerships between large organizational vendors. We often ask vendors to conduct specialty workshops on topics such as occupational safety and health administration (OSHA) training, accounting basics, and certified payroll. Many of the vendors, especially construction firms, have their own training programs that they willingly reconfigure so they can help other vendors—at no charge—particularly if they are actively doing business with the organization. An organization that is as committed to supplier development as it is to supplier diversity is bound to become an organization that consumers, employees, and business leaders alike will want to be a part of.

Renee Jones, MCA: Sr. Regional Diversity Director (SE), Skanska USA Building Inc.

I work for a global construction firm, and our supplier diversity plan looks very different depending on the market in which we are building. There are certain commonalities in every project, however. Whether we were starting a new project or managing one that will have us in a market for a number of years, we believe that our supplier diversity plan is essential for community stakeholder collaboration and for identifying the right community partner organizations. These collaborations help us develop a healthy education and development program that has the potential to impact the small business community long after a project is finished.

Trying to get started with external community partners or with industry-specific professional or trade organizations can be trying at best. The community organizations' expected outcomes do not always align perfectly with the priorities, mission, and objectives of the company. It is also easy to become overwhelmed with all of the various organizations that a diversity professional can join or support financially. Add in the myriad small business inclusion events, and the process can become downright exhausting.

When assessing an organization to determine if I should get involved, I use the process of elimination. I start by asking questions about the organization. How will it help me improve our supplier diversity program? Why should I choose this organization over another one? Determining if an organization is a good match for our business objectives greatly increases my ability to gain the buy-in and support of senior management and team members, who will have to become engaged with the organization. I work as the diversity lead in the southeast region of the United States in one of the world's leading construction and project development companies (we focus on select home markets in North America, Scandinavia, and other parts of Europe). During my time here, I have had the pleasure of forging relationships with numerous organizations, and I can tell you from experience that this strategy has been a winning formula for us.

Asking the Right Questions

When we embark on a new project or when we consider a new market where I am not familiar with the diverse business community, my team and I start by discussing and establishing our objectives. Then we go out and canvas the community to see what resources are available to help us achieve those objectives. Over the years, I have developed a pretty exhaustive evaluation process for determining the best partner(s) so that we can have the greatest impact in the community. I have found that it is better to do our due diligence up front so that we can avoid embarrassing or, worse, disappointing our client and failing to meet our goals. My team and I typically ask each other a host of questions, including the questions in these three areas:

Area 1: What do our client and the local leadership want to accomplish? Are there specific sectors of the subcontractor and supplier community we want to reach? Who is our target audience? Are we looking for general contractors, trade contractors, industry suppliers, or all of the above? Are we trying to engage minority firms in general or a particular sector of the community (e.g., black-, Hispanic-, LGBTQ-, or women-owned companies)?

Area 2: Consider the scope of the project: vertical or horizontal construction. Do we need firms that can perform locally, regionally, or nationally? Are our procurement processes inclusive, or are they difficult to navigate?

Area 3: Will this project have specific goals for MWBE participation? How have we performed on our most recent projects? Did we barely meet those goals or did we excel? Was there equity among all of the different categories (i.e., different trades or community sectors)? If not, we may have to reach out to a particular trade or community sector and perhaps help develop a more diverse business pool.

After determining our needs, I take a grassroots approach and comb the community for potential partner organizations that cater to the target audience(s) we are trying to engage. For example, when we are looking to connect with more American-Indian-owned firms, we look for tribal associations, chambers of commerce, or trade associations that have a strong American-Indian membership. My methodology for searching for businesses is deliberate and thorough. There are very few places I do not engage when I am on a mission to find firms. Here are a few resources that I find extremely helpful and are readily available, regardless of the geographic area:

Local government websites: If governments have small business programs, their websites will usually provide links to local and regional organizations that work with these businesses. I also try to establish a relationship with the government entities because they can become valuable resources, advocating for the project and directing firms to me.

Websites of national organizations: Also valuable are websites for organizations such as the National Association of Minority Contractors (NAMC), the National Minority Supplier Diversity Council (NMSDC), the Women's Business Enterprise National Council (WBENC), and the National Association of Women Business Owners (NAWBO). You can find information about local chapters and contacts and, if they exist, links to other minority organizations' websites. While I only listed organizations with a concentrated membership of minority- and women-owned business, there are many other helpful organizations that service construction professionals. These include the National Associations of Women in Construction (NAWIC), the National Society of

Black Engineers (NSBE), and the Society of Hispanic Professional Engineers (SHPE). Others can be found with a simple Google search.

Local chambers of commerce: They sometimes have committees or divisions that concentrate on MWBE recruitment, and they can usually tell you about organizations that service minority businesses in your area. Additionally, they can inform you of other chambers that represent specific communities, such as the American-Indian, Asian, or Hispanic communities.

Local minority media sources: These include newspapers or radio stations, especially those that target communities of color.

Local churches and advocacy groups: It is often a good idea to approach churches and organizations such as the NAACP, which usually have a firm grasp on business availability at the grassroots level.

Local conferences and events: Becoming visible at local community events is an excellent way to build rapport and trust with the business community. Events that take place during the Minority Enterprise Development Week (MED Week) are wonderful opportunities to show your support for the small business community. Dates of local and regional activities can be found at www.medweek.org.

Talking to the business community: Sometimes just speaking with minority- and women-owned subcontractors about any organizations and associations to which they belong can yield a lot of information, which can save you time and energy.

Narrowing Down

We cast a wide net to create a pretty extensive list of diverse suppliers, knowing that not every organization on the list is a good fit for partnership and that we will usually have to do some paring. The process of narrowing the list and selecting the partners that will provide the most value to us and to the project is not pleasant, but it is necessary. Here are a few suggestions when you sit down to narrow your list:

- Determine whether or not an organization aligns with your company's mission and vision statements. Figure out if their involvement will make your supplier diversity program stronger, allowing you to achieve the program's objectives.
- Try to determine if their goals and programs help their members increase capacity or provide some other form of development. If not, you might consider creating a development and business education program.

- If the organization offers certification for MWBE firms, is it a certification that you or your clients recognize and accept?
- Look at the constituency of the organization. Does it include the types of firms that you are looking to reach? Are the members actively engaged with the organization? Besides looking at the membership roster, you should also attend one or two of the organization's meetings or events to get a firsthand look at the membership and the level of participation.
- What are the chances of developing new relationships? If the goal is to meet new firms and you already know all of the members of an organization, you might consider having a different level of involvement with that organization.
- Who sits on an organization's executive board or advisory council? If any of your current or desired clients are involved, you will have additional incentive to align with the group.
- Look at the leadership and the structure already in place. Is the organization currently stable? Does it have an ongoing program? Will there be an immediate payoff in terms of connecting with your target audience, or will it require a great investment of time before firms are ready to do business with you? Depending on the financial and/or time resources you have available, it might be more advantageous to engage with an organization that can show an immediate return on investment.
- Ask about the financial commitment the organization is expecting. Will they require you to become a member? Are they expecting you to sponsor any of their events? If so, what are the sponsorship levels? No one wants to be caught off guard, especially when there is no budget attached to the project. Knowing the numbers ahead of time allows you to determine the best strategy for engaging the project team with the organization so they can see how they add value to your project.
- Evaluate the time commitment that will be required. What day does the organization meet? How long are the meetings? Which team members will attend the meetings? Will you be the only one participating? Will you be able to rotate attendance, or would you need to send a representative in your place? I have found that it is good to understand these details because you will only get out of the organization what you put in. It is not only important that the organization tries to meet your needs; you will have to make a realistic time commitment to get the best results and to build a relationship that is not just transactional.
- What does the training and education program offer the small businesses, specifically around capacity building and increasing business acumen? For example, are there support initiatives on which you can collaborate? Such initiatives might include the following:

- One-on-one coaching or executive relationships with similar functions
- Business process improvement and redesign, using lean processes
- Scholarships to MBEs for executive-level training or a similar program
- Small business finance options (e.g., lenders, mobilization, and equipment)
- Assistance in establishing joint ventures and valid strategic partnerships
- Technical assistance (e.g., marketing, management, accounting, operations, and human resources)

This narrowing process is very important, especially if the budget may not allow your company to participate in a way that the organization would like. Most of our clients like knowing what type of business education we will be providing to help MWBE firms, and we are often able to leverage the relationship. Establishing these partnerships has become a critical part of our strategic project pursuit plan, and it is a fantastic way to demonstrate our commitment to the local community and to strengthen the MWBEs with whom we hope to work.

Making the Relationship Work

Once I have decided on the right organization(s) with whom to partner, the real work begins. Although many of these relationships are established as a result of my organization's pursuit of a project in the market, I make sure that our partners know that we care about their success whether or not we win the project. I ultimately want to ensure that we will make a difference with the MWBEs in the community, beyond just paying dues or making a financial contribution to a group.

After an initial engagement with an organization, I try to meet with leaders to assess where I can have the greatest impact within their structure and within the community. I have come to learn that non-profits are often starving for guidance and have many needs beyond the purely financial. For those who ask for help, I step in and offer my expertise. I try to develop strong relationships with the leadership and with the other community stakeholders, which increase our visibility and help me determine if I want more involvement with them at another time. I also invite members of the partner organization to industry functions in which we participate or to educational programs we host. Maximizing any investment requires work, and it is these types of give-and-take relationships that help break down barriers and demonstrate that I am committed to making the relationships thrive.

When you begin engaging with small, community-based organizations, you will quickly discover that there is no shortage of requests for money for event sponsorship or ticket purchases—I am sure it does not help that I am a representative of a multinational construction firm—and it is important to put to rest certain misconceptions in order to keep the relationship progressing. Like every other supplier diversity program, I do not have an unlimited budget, and I am subject to financial limitations, shifts in priorities, process delays, and other constraints, all of which can make new financial commitments a challenge. And depending on how early we decide to enter a market and pursue a project, I may not have any budget at all to support any efforts, especially if we have not been awarded any work. These limitations require me to get savvy and to negotiate our involvement. I often have to demonstrate the value of, for example, a combination of monetary and in-kind contributions.

Even seemingly small gestures and in-kind contributions can be very beneficial to small organizations. Trainings at your facility can give you the opportunity to show your small business partners that their success is important to your company. Just think about the positive message you will send when you meet on a regular basis at your facility and interact with a team of community leaders, small business advocates, and small business owners. It demonstrates to both the community stakeholders and to your internal team that inclusion is very much part of the fabric of the organization. For me, there is no better feeling than accomplishing those two critical goals in one fell swoop. Here are some other examples of in-kind items or services that I have offered or regularly offer to our community partners:

- Conference room space for meetings.
- Marketing assistance such as the development of a brochure or a flyer for an organization's services or an upcoming event.
- Customized trainings for diverse businesses and/or leadership. This could include providing instructors or a guest speaker from my office or network.
- Process and back-office support.
- Conference call numbers for committee or board meetings.
- Photocopying or mailing for special events.
- Access to miscellaneous materials such as flip charts and easels. We might also lend a projector and a screen for important presentations.
- And, most importantly, time!

Communication Is Key

When I first started working with Skanska, one of my earliest mistakes was not communicating all of my activities to my leadership team and to clients in a format that was truly indicative of what I was doing. I routinely had casual chats with them, but I was not communicating the full breadth of my efforts. I soon came to realize that metrics speak volumes about your work and your successes. By learning to speak in metrics, I was able to protect my budget because I had the numbers that allowed me to properly justify my figures and to demonstrate the positive impact that my efforts were having in priming a community prior to our pursuit of a project.

As one of the first supplier diversity professionals at Skanska, I had no blueprint for managing the program. For communications, I had to learn what data they wanted to track, the format in which they wanted the information to be presented, and the frequency they wanted to receive it. Eventually, I developed an entire communications plan for senior leadership, which included quarterly project results and a quarterly newsletter that detailed activities, events, engagements, and awards or recognition. I also created an end-of-year supplier diversity report that outlined and measured our results against previous years, showing whether we had gains or losses. This plan became the standardized reporting plan for all Skanska supplier diversity units across the globe.

Communicating ROI

As with any company, when dollars are being spent, leadership will want to know the return on their investment, or ROI. The investment of time, energy, and resources is a vital part of an overall community development strategy. My leadership team appreciates both tangible and intangible benefits, and they often use both in other external marketing communications, extolling our program and our efforts in the community. My company frequently touts all of the following contributions to partner organizations:

- Number of interactions with current and future clients at organization events or at committee and board meetings.
- Number of times our company has been mentioned in the organization's marketing or communications (e.g., brochures, flyers, invitations, newsletters, or website pages).
- Number of MWBE members with whom you do business and, if possible, the cost savings or cost reduction these members brought to your company (you can show that the company would not have benefited from these savings if you had not met the MWBE at the organization. Many times these cost savings will more than pay for the membership cost of the organization).

- Organization scorecards to measure performance in meeting company objectives.
- Annual or quarterly MWBE spend reports that detail first- and second-tier levels.
- Number of small businesses added to our database.
- Number, if any, of scholarships provided. If they were provided, how many of those firms did business with us? What was our total spend with these firms?

Intangible results will require a little more thought and may vary by organization, but they are just as important as tangible results. When writing reports, I usually include my role within an organization, speaking engagements, workshop facilitation, or panel discussion participation, especially those panels that allow me to confirm my status as a subject-matter expert. I also include any awards that I receive on behalf of the company that recognize our efforts.

Working with community organizations has been a boon to my company, to our supplier diversity program, and to the small businesses that work with us. Not only have we found valuable MWBE partners with whom we work all over the country, but also we can show that we are truly willing to invest in the organizations that support the MWBE community. Many times, my company is the only resource available to these businesses for gaining the advantages necessary for future growth. In my business, the stability of the small business community is essential because it provides us with a pool of vendors for projects and equips MWBEs with a means for growing and expanding capacity. Sometimes businesses lament the amount of time that passes between their first meeting with us and an actual contract opportunity, but they must understand that we have a duty to our stakeholders to do our due diligence up front to ensure the success of a project. We are accountable to a host of people, sometimes for years before the project begins or after the project ends. It may take time to get the right fit, but this process is tried and tested, and it has yielded great professional and financial results for me and for my company.

A few years ago, I attended a Women's Business Summit in Alexandria, Virginia. I had the pleasure of meeting a very dynamic women-owned business and struck up a conversation with her. Instinctively (I've been doing this for a while), I could tell from our brief conversation that she had great business acumen and she was someone that could scale up to do business with a large corporation like the one I represented. I made arrangements to do a site visit and learn more about her firm to see if there were any opportunities for us to collaborate. To my joy, she did have an interest in working with a large firm and there were opportunities that were a good fit for her business. These were very small at the beginning and it took three years of coaching and mentoring on my part before she was able to secure her first sizeable contract. Since then, she has secured an additional three contracts with us totaling $1 million plus in revenue. It has been a joy to work with her and watch her firm grow. She is also officially one of our small business protégés in our executive management program and I know that she will be a great partner for us in the future.

Recalling another example, sometimes in our industry it is hard to find vendors that supply goods that are not brokers. A broker acts as a middleman to supply an item but does not necessarily produce it. For a cost, they facilitate delivery of that item to an end user. This itself is not bad business practice and, in actuality, is how many small businesses get their start and operate. However, when possible, my organization prefers to work as close to the actual supplier as possible. I had the opportunity to meet one such vendor at a vendor opportunity outreach meeting being held by one of our local small business agencies in North Carolina. This was truly a rare and phenomenal find for me as this young man had recently acquired a supplier that we routinely did business with. However, we were not aware that ownership had changed hands and that the company was not majority minority-owned (primary ownership control of more than 51% by a person identifying as a member of a minority group). Armed with this new and exciting information, we worked to get him certified as a minority vendor within the state of North Carolina. I reached out to my network of diversity professionals within the state who rallied behind him to ensure that this vendor would continue to be used under this new management. Because my territory extended as far north as Virginia, I also introduced him to our clients in the Virginia market by doing a live webinar of his facilities to show his scalability and capacity as a true supply vendor. With some advocacy teamwork, we were also able to get his firm certified in the state of Virginia. This immediately increased his revenue with the potential of additional $10 million forthcoming.

By helping this vendor navigate the system and connect to the right contacts, my firm was able to increase our diverse spend in Virginia $3 million plus. We have also added him as a protégé to our executive management program and are looking to extend his reach into the Florida market. Further, it demonstrates the impact that just one high-performing, scalable vendor can have of the diversity efforts for an organization and demonstrates the positive impact these efforts can have on organizations achieving their diversity spend goals.

Another example is one of persistence. We often tell our diverse vendors to be patient and persistent but that is important advice that also holds true for advocates. I met a diverse firm at a national supplier diversity event held in our local market in Virginia. He was definitely an up-and-coming trade contractor with an emphasis on sustainability which is a core value for my firm. We were able to do business with each other about a year after initially meeting and he did a good job that contract. Then there just did not seem to be another opportunity to work together for a number of years, which often happens in construction. However, we were both persistent. We followed up at least once a quarter and I kept his company profile up to date in our system, so if the right opportunity presented itself he would be ready. During this time, he also continued to work with other clients, keeping his business afloat and building his capacity. Finally, the right project came along and he stood ready and was awarded the contract. Currently, he has two contracts with us valued at around $2 million. We recently were just awarded another project that we pursued as a team (yes, multinational companies can partner with small businesses). This is yet another example of a diverse business that will be a long-term partner of ours going forward in the Virginia market.

Let's face it, going to an endless barrage of events can seem tedious and wearisome; however, it is the nature of the business. My advice is to definitely make it your aim to attend when your schedule permits *and* when you can be engaging. By presenting a positive demeanor, you will most likely attract the best and brightest of the small business attendees. If you are able to walk away with just one contact or, as I like to refer to them, gems, and with whom you can establish a long-term partnership, it will be well worth your time and effort. And you will be able to show positive return on investment of any funds you may have expended to be present. It will be that gem that keeps on shining in your organization that gives you the energy to search for the next success story.

Happy partnering!

10

Benchmarking, Quantifying, and Reporting: Measuring Success

From a corporate perspective, the success of a supplier diversity program goes far beyond an organization's diversity footprint. It has been well documented that a well-managed program does indeed deliver results and has a real and tangible economic impact. We all understand that the objective of a supplier diversity program is to ensure equity of procurement funds dispersed by an organization, but it is also important to understand the economic effects on the communities in which the programs operate. The human element of these programs should be at the forefront of everyone's mind in the supplier diversity community.

To measure, track, and report on the economic outcomes and effectiveness of a supplier diversity program, it is crucial that the data collected is valid and comes from a solid and trusted source. A good data plan allows a program to be assessed objectively. Further, the numbers should tell the story about how the program makes a difference in a community and about how much less robust that community would be without a program dedicated to giving diverse-owned suppliers the opportunity to provide value to an organization.

Data also allows reporting that is critical for understanding the mission of the program and identifying the success or failure of that mission. Think of the data that flows through the program as the lifeblood of the supplier diversity initiative. If the data flows smoothly, the initiative will have a higher likelihood of being healthy.

Data gathering involves tracking all aspects of every project involving an organization's diverse suppliers. This requires working with prime contractors to meet project goals based on which suppliers are available to perform the necessary work. When it comes to capturing the proper data, it is important that direct suppliers or prime contractors track the subcontractors that work on each project. This can be the most challenging aspect of a program because not all primes are devoted to supplier diversity. The most successful supplier diversity programs are those that work with partners who willingly share a similar mindset with their organization and view their relationship as a collaborative partnership.

Data collection can help prime contractors as well because they also need an effective way to identify all potential subcontractors capable of performing the work. Organizations can help facilitate this by playing matchmaker and putting the right suppliers on the radars of the prime contractors. By understanding their need gaps and utilizing two essential pieces of data such as certification codes and the commodity codes for each vendor, the data will advise on the level of qualification and address any pre-eligibility requirements.

An effective data collection plan will allow a program to generate insightful reports that will justify the program's efforts. This justification will always be required given that the program is a form of affirmative action. If reports demonstrate that the program is having a profound economic impact on the surrounding communities, the program will substantially increase its chances of survival. It is hard for executives to pull the plug on effective programs that are delivering positive results. Data will show the percentage of the funds to the suppliers and allow you to break those numbers down by dollar amount, by diversity participation and by the type of diverse-owned supplier. These numbers can be powerful allies.

Jaymie White, Diversity Reporting Solutions

It would be nice if an organization could pick up a how-to manual entitled something like *The Secrets to Building a Billion-Dollar Supplier Diversity Program* and know precisely how to go about building such a program, but the truth is that there are no shortcuts for growing a great program. It requires hard work, commitment, and corporate support.

Too often, companies create and maintain programs focused on connecting with diverse suppliers, absent of any specific strategy, taking what feels more like an "if we build it, they will come" approach. For savvy and experienced diverse suppliers, this lack of strategy usually demonstrates an absence of authentic commitment and typically results in stagnant and sometimes negative growth with diverse companies. Ultimately, this causes management to label their efforts a failure. Supplier diversity is a business strategy that, like all business strategies, requires clearly defined expectations and goals that will help a program grow until it becomes a corporate asset.

In my experience as a supplier diversity consultant and researcher, when it comes to benchmarking and establishing metrics for reporting, success factors encompass many variables and is dependent on several organizational factors such as the type of industry, stage of the program, that is, infancy, growing, mature, and so on. The principle that remains constant, regardless of any of these, is that it is essential for organizations to develop a set of realistic expectations so that stakeholders know what costs and benefits they can anticipate. Goals should connect with a company's policies so that they can be disseminated throughout the company. Additionally, they must receive support from corporate leadership; otherwise, they will have a limited impact in the long run. In addition to setting specific goals and expectations, a company must also create metrics for determining how to meet and, ideally, to exceed expectations.

Establishing Expectations and Goals

Corporations looking to increase their purchases with diverse suppliers need to be specific if they wish to create concrete change. One of the first steps in building a program is to scrutinize your current supply base in order to correctly develop a strategy for improving it. The following questions can help companies discover where they stand today:

- How will a supplier diversity program benefit your organization?
- What does your company consider a diverse supplier? Are certifications necessary?
- How many diverse suppliers do you have?
- How much are you spending with diverse suppliers?
- How much have you spent with diverse suppliers over the last one to five years?
- What is the spend breakdown by purchasing facility, department, or group?
- Whose responsibility is it currently to track diverse supplier information?

The more a company understands its current situation with diverse suppliers, the quicker it can proceed toward solutions that will benefit it over time. Following are a few questions that are best answered after examining a corporation's supply base situation:

- How is your company currently connecting with diverse suppliers?
- Where are these suppliers located?
- Are these suppliers primarily small or diverse?

Once these questions have been answered, the conversation can shift to goals and metrics. When crafting these goals and metrics, it is sensible to ask more in-depth questions that address specifics about data, growth, and overall program projections:

- What was the company's percent of change in the number of diverse suppliers over the last two years? Five years?

  – Per facility, department, or group?

- What was the company's percent of change in spending with diverse suppliers over the last two years? Five years?

  – Per facility, department, or group?

- Based on the company's supplier database, what is the projected growth rate for the number of diverse suppliers and the spend with those suppliers over the next two years? Five years? Ten years?

  – Is the number of diverse suppliers and the spend with those suppliers consistent with the company's goals? For example, if the company spends the bulk of its purchases with manufacturing suppliers, is this reflected in the diverse supplier base?
  – If not, why?

- Where are the available diverse suppliers geographically located—locally, regionally, statewide? Can this number be increased? Should it be increased?
- How has the company connected with diverse suppliers in the past? How will the company do so in the future? What are the primary ways that diverse suppliers receive their information, for example, email, print, and social media.
- Which bids have these suppliers participated in or won over the past year? Two years?

  – What bids are upcoming over the next year? Two years?

- What groups should be engaged or joined in order to connect with more diverse suppliers?

  – How many suppliers are you looking to connect with through these groups over the next two years? Five years? Ten years?
  – How will this affect the organization's spend? How should it affect the spend?

After answering these questions, there should be enough data available to develop goals that are specific, realistic, attainable, and measurable in order to grow the program.

Disparity Studies

The process of creating goals can be very controversial and contentious, particularly in communities with a history of systemic disparities in equitable procurement practices. Corporations in the private sector have more flexibility in this area and their efforts are guided by consumers, the community, and stakeholders. However, supplier diversity programs in the public sector are greatly influenced and impacted by goal setting. In order to develop goals that are specific, realistic, attainable, and measurable, many entities endeavor to commission their own disparity study or partner with other local agencies for a joint disparity study as the basis for and justification of their supplier diversity program and efforts.

A disparity study determines whether a government entity, either in the past or currently, engages in exclusionary practices in the solicitation and award of contracts to minority, and women-owned, and disadvantaged business enterprises. These studies help to determine if there is a disparity between the availability of firms and the utilization of those firms in the market area. Disparity studies were necessitated in part by the 1989 US Supreme Court's decision in the case of *City of Richmond v. J.A. Croson*. The court decision imposed legal requirements on jurisdictions to establish a "compelling interest" to support the establishment of a minority and women business program.

While there are many factors that impact whether a disparity exists, disparity is usually calculated in the form of an index called the disparity index. The disparity index is a ratio of the percentage of utilization and the percentage of available diverse firms. If the disparity index is 100, the utilization of diverse firms is leveled with the availability of diverse firms in the designated market area. If the index is less than 80, it indicates that diverse firms are significantly underutilized by an entity based on availability.

I have seen numerous goal setting formulas, ranging from simple equations to mathematical calculations that look like something from a quantum physics textbook. However, in my experience, the best formulas are those that are the easiest to decipher and explain. This is especially important in the public sector as all it takes is for one bid award to be challenged due to a perceived lack of fairness or transparency of the goal setting process, for a program to be rendered race and gender neutral, or, worse, totally disbanded.

The process for establishing goals is one that should not be done hastily. It is a deliberate process and appropriate time should be given to address and answer the previously posed questions. The more specific the goals, the easier it will be to establish objectives that will result in successful outcomes in the organization's supplier diversity initiative. Further, it will allow for the goals to be defended if challenged or questioned. One of the reasons programs are shut down or adopt a race/gender-neutral status is because the goals and practices of the program were deemed questionable or unfair and could not be justified based on specific data.

Ultimately, establishing diverse spending goals should align with the organization's procurement strategy and take into account the current availability of diverse businesses while addressing the historical disparities of the past.

Action Plan

After establishing goals for a supplier diversity program, the next step is to formulate a plan executing those goals. Keep in mind that connecting with diverse suppliers affects the entire supply base. Separating supplier diversity program goals from overall procurement goals can harm the program if that metric is perceived as less important than procurement numbers. Ideally, the supplier diversity strategy that is adopted and set in motion will be connected to the organization's overall procurement strategy.

It is essential to delineate responsibilities within the organization company to create accountability. It is also imperative to develop a consistent tracking mechanism to pinpoint each metric and to determine how best to achieve success. This is especially important if an organization has high turnover rates. It is helpful to identify who will complete reports and how often they will be compiled and submitted for review to confirm program progress. Today, many leading supplier diversity programs have analysts whose primary function is to analyze diverse spend data. Presenting a report for review by a department head is a good way to maintain movement toward the target as well as demonstrate the efforts of the program. Some of the metrics tracked include tracking the goal by specific departments, classification (e.g., minority-owned, veteran-owned, or women-owned), or location in an attempt to better understand organizational strengths, weaknesses, and future opportunities. Utilizing a manual entry or a third-party system may be necessary to keep the process consistent.

Once internal processes are set, external strategies can be created. Understanding what networks to build and how best to build them is another important step in developing a successful program. Researching and connecting with organizations that advocate for the advancement of diverse suppliers can help a company create better ways to grow its supply base. Another great way to improve supplier diversity effectiveness is to encourage employees to join industry organizations so they can connect with experienced supplier diversity professionals.

Quantifying and Reporting

This is where the proverbial rubber meets the road. Managing the performance of a supplier diversity program is crucial to its success. Below are a few key performance indicators that can help facilitate effective program management. There are few supplier diversity programs that track every one of these measures, but most programs track several of these. Determining what works best, again, depends on the organization's overall procurement strategy and the goals and objectives for the program. The below Table 10.1 outlines some common performance measures to ensure that the supplier diversity program is operating toward maximum optimal and quantifiable outcomes.

Table 10.1 Performance measures

Performance measure	Description
Baseline measurement	• The first step in utilizing metrics effectively is to identify your program's supplier portfolio and to establish baseline data • Knowing where your supplier program is going is difficult if you do not know where it is presently • Establishing a baseline with the help from data enrichment gives you a starting point from which supplier diversity can grow
Diverse spend	• This metric is a measure of how much money your company is spending with diverse suppliers • It is the building block for many other metrics • It is easily trackable month over month and year over year • While diverse spend often acts as a cornerstone metric, many companies put more weight on different analytics when measuring total supplier diversity success
Diverse count	• This is a measure of how many diverse suppliers you contract rather than the overall spend to those suppliers • Diverse count may be more critical than spend to your supplier diversity program's success • Programs that are dependent on the diverse spend of just a few suppliers, the numbers can take a tumble if one or two drop out, which happens more frequently with small business • By measuring diverse count along with diverse spend, you will be better positioned to weather the storm if you suddenly lose a key diverse supplier

(continued)

Table 10.1 (continued)

Performance measure	Description
Economic impact	• This metric is great because it focuses on the ripple effects of your supplier diversity program, that is, how many jobs have been created as a result of your efforts? How has your program impacted local economies? • Besides measuring success, the data provides hard evidence to prove the value of your supplier diversity initiative to the C-suites and the community at large
Cost savings	• While this tends to be more of a procurement metric, supplier diversity programs can save money, both in terms of a stronger supply chain and in terms of government incentives realized • Measuring cost savings shows how much your efforts are improving the organization's bottom line
Revenue impact	• This metric shows how relationships with diverse suppliers have affected organization's revenue and revenue forecasts
Market share	• This measurement analyzes how much your supplier diversity program helped increase market share and market penetration within diverse communities
Deals won	• This is a tally of how many diverse suppliers were contracted over a certain time period • This information can also be combined with the number of diverse suppliers who left the portfolio to arrive at net data
Deals lost	• This is often due to a myriad of factors • However, losing a lot of deals may suggest that strategies for identifying and contracting diverse suppliers might need tweaking
Tier II performance	• This is a measurement—both spend and count—of the supplier diversity efforts of your direct suppliers or prime contractors, whether they are diverse or non-diverse • Because Tier II is an increasingly competitive way to compute overall diverse spend, this metric takes on added importance for any organization looking to take its supplier diversity program to the next level

Tier I and Tier II Spending

In the competitive global market, it is more important than ever that firms have a laser focus on their core competencies, hence the rise in outsourcing non-essential functions and subcontracting. It is far more cost effective for several companies to specialize in making certain components than for one company to generate and market products end-to-end. Also called direct or indirect spending, Tier I or Tier II spending allows companies to narrow their focus on one aspect, thus ensuring they have the necessary resources available, have the best teams in place to perform, and oft times, can offer cost savings to their customers. This spend is also increasingly routinely reviewed and analyzed as organizations look to ensure their values and best practices are being espoused by their large, prime strategic partners.

Typically, Tier I companies offer the most advanced processes in the supply chain and are best suited to financially accommodate the full scope of a project or fulfill an order, and so on. Tier II companies are suppliers who, although no less vital to the supply chain, are usually limited in what they can produce. These companies are usually smaller and have less technical advantages than Tier I companies; however, they can be vital to the success of a Tier I firm. Let's take, for example, a large construction project. Most organizations have adopted a construction management approach to managing large, complex construction projects, hiring a prime or Tier I contractor to manage the construction of the building. Depending on the organization and the contract, the Tier I or prime is limited in the amount of work they are actually allowed to perform on the project, thus, they are required to subcontract a substantial portion or majority of the work out to subcontractors or Tier II firms.

A project may have many more tiers than this, including Tier III, Tier IV, and so on, depending on the scale and complexity of the project. However, the relationship between Tier I and Tier II companies shows how all of them operate—Tier II generates and supplies Tier I with the products it needs to generate and supply the OEM with what is needed for the final products. The supply chain is only as strong as its weakest company link, so having healthy business practices is important for every tier to keep in operation.

There is no magic wand for creating or improving your supplier diversity program. Success demands a business strategy to ensure positive progress and growth. This strategy should be linked to corporate policies and to overall procurement goals, and it must be backed by leadership in order to flourish. Centering goals around current diverse supplier data is absolutely necessary for determining what success looks like. It is also essential to assign responsibilities for supplier diversity information and to determine how best to track and report the program goals. Finally, it is vital that companies identify and connect with organizations that can help their respective program grow.

Part V

The Future of Supplier Diversity Programs

11

The "New" Business Case

The US Census Bureau has repeatedly confirmed that consumers are becoming more diverse, and companies are taking notice. Ford Motor Company, for example, has been a leader in supplier diversity spending in the automotive industry for years. Ford also benefits from the diverse thinking and fresh ideas born from these relationships. Ford's diverse suppliers have provided substantial contributions to its growth in the form of new product and technology development, from sustainable products to fuel-efficient vehicle technologies. Ford recognizes how vital small and minority-owned businesses are to the US economy and to the identity of the Ford Motor Company. Ford understands and promotes within its company the direct and positive economic impact that minority business procurement has on the communities where it does business. For them, investing in these minority-owned businesses helps build brand loyalty from the companies and communities that directly benefit from the jobs and the wealth created by their investment in supplier diversity.

Companies that engage in socially responsible business practices appeal to a broad market of socially conscious consumers interested in supporting companies that make a difference in communities. According to a recent Edelman Goodpurpose study, "87% of global consumers believe businesses should place equal weight on both societal issues and business issues." By investing in suppliers with diversity programs, companies can attract these socially conscious consumers because the extent of a company's investment in its supplier diversity program reflects the company's commitment to progressive business. In addition, these companies often extract other benefits, including increased market share and access to new revenue opportunities.

© The Author(s) 2019

K. K. Porter, *Implementing Supplier Diversity*, https://doi.org/10.1007/978-3-319-94394-7_11

Research by companies like The Hackett Group (NASDAQ: HCKT) challenges the conventional mindsets of many business leaders, who worry that dedicating resources to supplier diversity will divert attention from other strategic activities. Laura Gibbons, the research director for The Hackett Group, says that:

> Supplier diversity is evolving from a check-the-box corporate social responsibility requirement to a strategic enabler providing access to innovative products and increased market share in new and developing communities. Top-performing organizations are taking advantage of this opportunity and applying the tenets of social diversity to new areas such as supplier partnering, reputation management and global expansion with exceptional results.

To unlock the full potential benefits of supplier diversity efforts, The Hackett Group recommends that companies consider expanding beyond traditional goals such as complying with regulations. Top performers in supplier diversity recognize the value in objectives like gaining access to new markets and improving supplier partnerships. Companies should also look beyond basic measures like percentage of spend with diverse suppliers and calculate the true value of supplier diversity by using more sophisticated performance metrics like satisfaction levels and other secondary metrics that are aligned with long- and short-term plans and objectives.

Research shows that companies with top-performing supplier diversity programs focus on several areas in order to make the most of their efforts. These companies tend to have a strong business development push, whether it is developing supplier partnerships, mentoring local suppliers, or collaborating with suppliers on product innovation. They use supplier diversity as a customer reputation management (CRM) tool to help increase market share and attract and retain talent. They also actively educate internal stakeholders in order to create a culture that values supplier diversity while interacting with the local communities of suppliers and consumers to better understand the market, establish relationships, and support supplier diversity goals.

While most supplier diversity programs have a domestic focus, The Hackett Group's research finds that more than 40% of all global companies with a US supplier diversity program plan to expand globally within the next two to three years. The Hackett Group recommends that companies manage US and global programs as a single initiative, where appropriate. It is also highly advisable to partner with corporate diversity groups that manage workforce diversity and to work with third parties that can help companies connect with diverse suppliers.

Scott Vowels, Supplier Diversity Expert and Author

Many thousands of years ago, when the ancient Greeks sought to determine what the future held, they consulted the high priestess of the temple of Apollo, Pythia, better known as the Oracle at Delphi. These days we do not put much stock in oracles. Instead, we consult historians, journalists, university professors, and industry experts when we want to know what the future holds. For more than two decades, I have talked and worked with supplier diversity experts to understand the changing landscape of supply chains. While the consensus in the supplier diversity community is that the future of supplier diversity lies down the path of developing the new business case, there are several ideas that should be addressed to better allow the industry to understand the value that it brings to organizations.

As a supplier diversity historian, researcher, and practitioner at one of the world's leading and technology companies and one of the most forward-thinking brands, the future is at the heart of everything that we do. We focus not just on what's now, but what's next … and what's next after that. Here are my thoughts on what's next for supplier diversity and what the "new" business case will need to look like in order for the industry to continue to thrive and remain relevant in the future:

- Advocacy groups focusing on collaboration and simplification
- Diverse suppliers incorporating strategic partnerships and focusing on pipeline development
- Industry leveraging and embracing technology and analytic tools
- Organizations shifting beyond the "PO (purchase order) push" and embracing a strategic sourcing focus

Advocacy Groups Focusing on Collaboration and Simplification

Not too long ago at a symposium entitled "The Bigger Discussion V: Future of Supplier Diversity," leaders from four of the nation's most recognized certification agencies gathered for the first time ever to discussion the future of diverse supply chains in front of a packed auditorium. The illustrious panel included Louis Green, interim president of the National Minority Supplier Development Council (NMSDC); Pamela Prince-Eason, CEO of the Women's Business Enterprise National Council (WBENC); Justin Nelson, president of the

National LGBT Chamber of Commerce (NGLCC); and Keith King, president of the National Veteran Business Development Council (NVBDC).

Although each of the organizations represented on the panel was founded to support a specific demographic within the world of business development and supplier diversity, each leader acknowledged that the challenges of each organization are very similar. One unifying belief was that they could all do a better job of collaborating with like-mined, non-governmental organizations (NGOs) to advance ideas and best practices. A prime example of a healthy supplier diversity-NGO collaboration is the recently created National Business Inclusion Consortium (NBIC) Best-of-the-Best Awards. The purpose of these awards is to recognize outstanding achievement in the promotion of cross-segment diversity and inclusion, both within the diverse supplier community and within corporation, helping to identify and help model supply diversity success.

In February 2011, the Small Business Administration (SBA) implemented the Women-Owned Small Business (WOSB) federal contract program with the goal of expanding the opportunities for WOSBs to win federal contracts by providing a level playing field. It is also intended to help federal agencies meet their contracting goals for WOSBs, allowing them to vie for competitive set-asides or to apply for sole-source set-asides in industries where women-owned small businesses are substantially underrepresented. I think it is important to note that in 2016, the federal government spent $19.6 billion with WOSBs, much of which was disbursed through competitive or sole-source set-asides.

In 2016, the federal government also reported spending $100 billion with small businesses, $39.1 billion with small disadvantaged businesses, $16.3 billion with service-disabled veteran-owned small businesses, and $6.9 billion with HUBZone businesses. All told, the federal government spent $182 billion with these diverse suppliers in 2016, including WOSBs.

The federal government also has a similar program for veterans through the VETS First Verification Program, also called the Veteran's First Contracting Program. This program is administered through the Veteran's Administration and is accepted as a certification on federal solicitations.

These are both good starts and the federal government has a number of classifications for small business inclusion. However, they lack any cohesiveness or connectivity with other organizations outside the federal government, making the ability to secure one of these contracts complicated and a long shot at best. A step toward stronger and simpler collaboration would be to offer contract programs that advance competitive or sole-source set-asides to other demographics, including LGBT-owned small businesses or minority-owned small businesses, with the certifications administered by the appropriate certifying agencies, that is, NGLCC (LGBT businesses), NMSDC (minority businesses), or NVBDC (veteran-owned businesses).

Diverse Suppliers Incorporating Strategic Partnerships and Focusing on Pipeline Development

For years, supplier diversity professionals have been encouraging businesses to pursue strategic partnerships as the key to scaling quickly and bringing more value to the clients and customers that they serve. In the for-profit world, a first-class strategic partnership or alliance can give a business a competitive advantage and access to an array of resources and expertise. Associations, alliances, and NGOs should use a similar paradigm moving forward into the future and must begin to use the methods that allow large businesses to succeed. In order for these partnerships to be effective, the work being done, the benefits accrued from that work, and the risk involved from said partnership must be spread equitably among the partners. I have seen too many strategic alliances fail because one partner takes on the lion's share of the labor while other partners sit idly by and reap the benefits of someone else's work or, worse, a firm goes out of business after a strategic partnership. Strategic partnerships yield benefits when each partner delivers on the promise of excellence in that partner's particular area of expertise, both financially and professionally.

Pipeline development is important from both the practitioner perspective and the minority supplier/vendor perspective. Pipeline programs are an investment in the future. In order for programs to be successful, there has to be a constant pool of vendors that are ready and available to do business with organizations. Maintaining a steady flow of businesses is even more critical, as minority businesses tend to be more susceptible to market fluctuations and the general challenges of entrepreneurship, causing them to drop out of the supply chain at a much higher rate than other businesses. While a definitive number on how many small businesses closed during the 2008 recession is hard to come by, minority businesses were disproportionately impacted, with many entering into new industries, reemerging as scaled-back versions or closing altogether and never returning to the marketplace.

Pipeline development is also important for the practitioner side, as the industry will continue to need trained and dedicated professionals that are committed to helping businesses succeed while continuing to push the industry forward. Presently, there is no clear path to a career in supplier diversity. Colleges do not offer a formal curriculum or classes on supplier diversity industry, with most practitioners learning on the job. Over the years, advocacy groups have sought to fill this gap, creating a number of independent educational opportunities across the country. As the industry has evolved, the tools have become more sophisticated, and organizational outcomes have gotten more imperative, the need for industry professionals is greater than ever.

Industry Leveraging and Embracing Technology and Analytic Tools

How will technology change the look of your workforce? This simple question does not have a simple answer. Most of my Millennial and iGeneration (a.k.a. Generation Z or the Homeland Generation) friends have trouble even conceptualizing a 9-to-5 job. Thousands of articles have been written about ways to assimilate Millennials into the workforce, but less has been said about the best methods for integrating the iGeneration, a generation that could make or break supplier diversity. According to some demographic experts, the iGeneration is made up of people born between 1995 and 2012, which means that many people in this generation have no concept of a world without smartphones or social media. These technologies are simply a way of life for them.

Besides being the most technologically astute generation in US history, the iGeneration will also be the most diverse generation. According to the US Census Bureau, 50.2% of children under the age of 18 will be part of a minority race or ethnic group by 2020.

Whether you like it or not, in the next five to ten years, the iGeneration will be entering the workforce en masse. This generation wants to be paid a fair wage while doing meaningful work in an environment that allows them to grow their skillsets. They are bringing a completely different set of capabilities, needs, and desires with them. Successful diverse businesses must begin preparing for the iGeneration as soon as possible if they want to remain competitive and be relevant in the future.

Organizations Shifting Beyond the "PO Push" and Embracing a Strategic Sourcing Focus

As supplier diversity is inextricably intertwined with an organization's procurement activities, any discussion of the future of supplier diversity must include a discussion on the future of the supply chain. The supply chain (whether diverse or not) is not static, it is a work in progress. Over the last ten years, most major corporate procurement organizations have undergone a transformation in responsibilities, which has been driven by the need to be more strategic, by the need to collaborate better with suppliers and customers, and by rapidly changing technology. However, it is still near-impossible to find procurement organizations that do not look much different from the organizations of the past, whose sole function seems to be to process purchase orders (POs).

For a procurement organization focused on churning out POs, actionable relationships are practically non-existent and the antithesis of the supplier diversity function, which, at its core, is about building relationships. Supplier diversity professionals working within a PO-driven organization must decipher ways to get around this entrenched mentality by getting to know the buying community and establishing themselves as capable and trusted resources for providing competent, quality suppliers. But supplier diversity professionals must understand that they are only as good as their last referral, which means that it is essential to vet diverse suppliers before presenting them as viable options to the PO pusher. This is where a strong business development program becomes essential.

As with anything, there are advantages and disadvantages of working with a PO pusher. The upside of working with a buyer whose sole concern is getting the PO processed and moving on to the next one as quickly as possible is that once a diverse supplier has established itself as a reliable, go-to entity, the PO pusher will more than likely return for repeat business. The secret to getting in good with a PO pusher is to get that first order right. The PO pusher seeks efficiency in their job and in their suppliers, so dot your i's and cross your t's on that first order, and the PO pusher will be hooked. You also likely will not need to bid against other suppliers for the next order. The downside of working with a PO pusher is that there is no time for supplier development or strategic engagement between the diverse supplier and the buying entity. The buyer processing the PO simply wants to know that the order will be where it is supposed to be and when it is supposed to be there. While we reference some of our procurement colleagues as PO pushers in jest, it is not a joke that this type of environment becomes transactional and may not allow the vendor to develop the knowledge and skills necessary to build a long-term business relationship.

Obviously not all companies employ only PO pushers. Some companies continually evolve their supply chain management practices to keep pace with increased cost pressures and competition from the marketplace. According to the authors of the Oxford Report, the trend for forward-thinking companies is to challenge their supply chain organizations to find more innovative ways to drive costs down by partnering with suppliers who can bring maximum value to a company. The authors of the Vision 2020 report predict that the two core tenets of the future of supply chain management will be the widening strategic scope of procurement and the growing importance of collaboration with suppliers and other departments within a business. Most of the supply chain executives surveyed for the Oxford Report corroborate this prediction, saying that they see procurement within their companies and more collaborations with additional suppliers as playing an increased strategic role in their companies.

Rather than negotiating for better pricing on one-off deals, forward-thinking suppliers are often being brought in earlier in the design phase to help the buying organization realize cost savings and to take advantage of the supplier's innovation. In cases where there is no intellectual property at stake, the partnering supplier can walk away with a new product—already user-tested—that it can sell to other customers. This kind of strategic collaboration with the supplier represents a big leap forward for the procurement/supply chain process at most companies and a dramatic change in the relationship between major buying organizations and their suppliers. If this is the future of supply chain management, then the future will be bright for supplier diversity.

According to the authors of reports published by The Hackett Group and ConnXus ("The Business Case for Supply Chain Sustainability Through Strategic Supplier Inclusion"), companies that have actively involved small and diverse-owned businesses in their procurement processes have in many cases reported leaner, more sustainable, and more innovative supply chains. In fact, companies with more robust supplier diversity programs have reported increased profitability, upward of 133% return on procurement investment

> The SBA reports that 99.7% of all US firms are small businesses and that minority- and women-owned companies represent more than 50% of the total small business population. Within the next several decades, the United States will become a minority-majority country, so it stands to reason that when major buying organizations are looking for suppliers with whom they can partner and collaborate, they will often be looking to the community of diverse-business owners.

The future is already upon us and what we know for sure is that understanding the past can help to dictate our steps. As we enter into what is inevitably going to be described as the next era of supplier diversity, you may find that the "new" business case will rely on good, old-fashioned tactics from the past.

12

From Social Issue to Business and Economic Imperative: The Impact of Changing Demographics

According to the US Census Bureau, more than half of all Americans will belong to a minority group by the year 2044. This major demographic shift will have a significant impact on every aspect of the country. Improving minority access to business opportunities will be more than a social issue; it will be an economic imperative. Because entrepreneurship and small business ownership are the greatest drivers of wealth and job creation in the United States, access to employment and entrepreneurship among minorities in the future will be exponentially more important to the health and sustainability of the US economy.

In today's fiercely competitive global business environment, organizations are faced with a harsh new reality: The antiquated supply chains of yesteryear are no longer sufficient for addressing the relentlessly shifting demographics within the marketplace or for capturing a qualified cohort of uniquely talented, diverse professionals. Shifting demographics and related business growth rates now demand a fresh approach for creating a robust, inclusive, and responsive talent pipeline, making supplier diversity a must for businesses. Consequently, companies are relying on diverse supply chains now more than ever to add value and to deliver strategic cost savings that impact the bottom line.

As the makeup of the US population shifts dramatically toward increased diversity, companies must address a consumer base that is anything but homogenous. Dr. Fred McKinney, former managing director of minority business programs at the Dartmouth College Tuck School of Business, believes that the changing demographics of consumer markets is the most important reason to implement supplier diversity programs. He argues that "The issue of diversity is something that any senior executive ignores at their peril. Supplier

© The Author(s) 2019
K. K. Porter, *Implementing Supplier Diversity*, https://doi.org/10.1007/978-3-319-94394-7_12

diversity is connected to market diversity because people do care what these companies do and the impact that they have in their communities." He also adds that "Companies that are not just selling to, but also buying from communities of color—who have been largely left out of the corporate industrial landscape until more recently—will benefit if they are doing this well."

Just as the demographics of the consumer markets are changing, so too is the makeup of the labor markets. As more minorities and women come into positions of corporate power, they are asking their companies and their employees about their commitments to minority businesses and communities. A 2010 study from the Center for Creative Leadership found that "The higher an employee rates their organization's corporate citizenship, the more committed they are to the organization." The reality is that the global business environment is growing more complex and diverse every day. If individuals and organizations fail to understand this truth and do not govern themselves accordingly, their capacity to be effective players in the marketplace will be limited.

Harvard University is a prime example of a higher education institution that has paid close attention to this shift and has made clear its commitment to supplier diversity on its campus. Harvard's strategic procurement process reveals its insightful approach to securing corporate procurement and to implementing sourcing procedures that benefit all participants in the supply chain's ecosystem. It is worth highlighting the focused purchasing process employed by Harvard, which leads by example and leverages its influence in the following ways to promote awareness and support for a more diverse supply chain:

- Promoting inclusive procurement across schools and business units.
- Informing schools and business units about the benefits of inclusive procurement and sharing best practices.
- Educating vendors about the Harvard environment and how to conduct business at the university.
- Establishing processes to help the purchasing community identify diverse and small vendors who are ready, willing, and able to conduct business with Harvard.
- Encouraging preferred vendors to develop a Tier II supplier diversity program.
- Increasing awareness around regulatory mandates that focus on supplier diversity.
- Providing opportunities for diverse vendors and members of the Harvard purchasing community to meet and build relationships.

- Establishing reporting and monitoring capabilities to track against targets.
- Identifying high-probability sourcing opportunities and prequalifying diverse businesses for inclusion in the bid process.
- Representing Harvard in the business community.

On the corporate side, DuPont has also made a strong commitment to supplier diversity. For 45 years, it has had a "formal commitment to supplier diversity as an essential business strategy that recognizes the economic advantages of tapping into the strength of small and diverse suppliers and of helping create strong economies." No wonder it has continued to expand and excel over the years.

CVS Health is yet another company that has been proactive in diversifying its supply chain. Each year it delivers healthcare services in all 50 US states and touches the lives of 100 million people, all of whom have unique needs and backgrounds. They note that "As our country's demographics change and our patient and customer population becomes increasingly diverse, we are keeping pace by diversifying our workforce and supply chain."

Harvard University, DuPont, and CVS Health are standout examples of shifting mindsets and intelligent processes at work. When supplier diversity programs are carefully created and monitored, they can deliver measurable returns on their investments. Many other companies, however, are coming up short, even those that have the best of intentions. It is not enough to make superficial claims about "diversity and inclusion" on social media or in annual reports. To be a leader in supplier diversity, an organization must put its money where its mouth is.

The Growth of Minority Business

Over the past ten years, minority-owned businesses have grown at approximately double the rate of all firms in the United States. There are more than two million minority firms in the United States that generate in excess of $205 billion in annual sales. Between 1997 and 2002, roughly 50% of the growth of all firms came from minority businesses alone. There are already more than a thousand US-based information technology (IT) companies owned by women and minorities, ranging from startups to mature companies with annual revenues north of $100 million. Most of these firms operate across national borders and in several IT disciplines.

Minority Spending Power

Between 1990 and 1997, the buying power of African American, Hispanic, and Asian communities rose by 54%, 58%, and 72%, respectively. In 2000, the total purchasing power in the United States was more than $6.5 trillion, and white, non-Hispanics accounted for nearly 80% of that purchasing power. That number will drop significantly as minority purchasing power rises from approximately 20% in 2000 to more than 45% by the year 2045. In 2015, minority purchasing power surpassed $2 trillion; it is expected to reach $3 trillion by 2030. These pockets of demand have considerable profit potential for companies. Current estimates indicate that at least 30% of inner-city retail demand is unmet, which translates into approximately $25 billion in unrealized sales. There is considerable room for growth in these areas.

Magic Johnson Enterprises is one company that is working hard to bring business opportunities to underserved urban communities. Founded and run by the former NBA star Earvin "Magic" Johnson, the company has enjoyed remarkable success in many inner cities, in part by bringing franchises such as Starbucks, TGI Friday's, and Burger King into these areas. Through strategic alliances, Magic Johnson and Johnson Development Corporation (JDC) have combined critical market knowledge and the ability to identify areas with sales potential. The results have been quite impressive.

JDC provides entertainment complexes, restaurants, and retail centers to underserved markets across the country. The company has 50/50 partnerships with several of the most successful businesses in their market categories and has more than 100 Starbucks, 30 Burger Kings, and 26 home loan centers, all of which provide more than 15,000 jobs to minorities. This type of strategic alliance is important because as traditional domestic markets become saturated and companies merge, growth will be a challenge for both large companies and smaller minority firms. Exploring new markets is essential for continued prosperity and growth.

The world's biggest retailer, Walmart, is also achieving gains by working closely with diverse suppliers. The retail giant spent more than $3.9 billion with nearly 2000 minority-owned suppliers in 2007 and used community outreach to help develop suppliers. In 2006, Walmart held the Minority Construction Summit, which included sessions for minority construction firms interested in building new stores, remodeling existing stores, and conducting facility maintenance programs. Since then, Walmart has held more than nine sessions about how to do business with the company. These sessions are part of a nationwide initiative to help small businesses grow and to foster economic opportunity in neighborhoods in need. Walmart also gave executives at local chambers of commerce training and best practice tools to contribute to the success of local Hispanic-owned businesses. As a result, when Hispanic businesses scale up, Walmart is able to rely upon them to meet customer needs. For example, Ruiz Foods, the largest Mexican frozen food company in the United States, is one of Walmart's largest domestic product suppliers. According to Lee Scott, then president and CEO of Walmart, "As part of our continuing effort to become a leader in diversity, we will increase the amount of business we do with minority companies, using our size and leverage to create companies of size and stature."

Good things are also happening in the world of information technology. IBM is the first information technology company to spend more than $1 billion with minority businesses. In 2007, the company spent $2.3 billion with diverse companies in business services, facility management, travel, and technical subcontracting. One strategy the company uses to promote diverse suppliers is to match minority suppliers with IBM executives or managers through a mentoring program that lasts 12–18 months. The program speaks volumes about IBM's priorities.

The minority population of the United States is increasing in size, purchasing power, and business development activity. This record growth is enabling minorities to wield significant economic power as consumers and business owners. Their clout positions them to be invaluable strategic suppliers and business partners in the years ahead. Forward-thinking companies have recognized this truth and are implementing well-laid supplier diversity plans to stay ahead. Successful plans consider organizational culture, senior-level commitment, strategic alignment, and appropriate risk-taking. Strategic alliances with diverse suppliers have also shown significant promise. These alliances have the potential to pay huge dividends down the road.

Global Impact

While supplier diversity is entrenched domestically and is light years ahead of international markets in terms of creating opportunities for diverse businesses, and formal processes that connect businesses to opportunities, the growth potential of global markets presents another reason supplier diversity has become an economic imperative. As international markets continue to expand, in size and diversity, they are increasingly intrigued by the organization of resources and the results achieved in the United States. Many countries have sought to replicate US supplier inclusion programs, with several countries starting their own programs or creating alliances with domestic advocacy and certifying groups such as the Canadian Aboriginal and Minority Supplier Council, Minority Supplier Development in China, Minority Supplier Development UK (MSDUK), Supply Nation (Australia), and the South African Supplier Diversity Council. These groups present opportunities not only to the business communities that they serve but also to US diverse businesses looking to do business internationally.

Research by The Hackett Group found that more than 40% of all global companies with a US supplier diversity program plan to expand globally within the next two to three years. The Hackett Group recommends that companies manage US and global programs as a single initiative, where appropriate.

One such company with a strong take on international supplier diversity is IBM. According to Michael Robinson, Program Director—Global Supplier Diversity for IBM, "At IBM, we've been leading the way in corporate supplier diversity efforts for nearly 50 years. We are the only company that, we know of, has a diverse supplier requirement in every country where we operate worldwide. We count on our supplier network, and ask the same thing of our women- and minority-owned suppliers as we do of our majority suppliers … that they help us provide value to the customer, strengthen our brand, understand our markets, and identify what's coming next in the world of technology. It's in our best interest to find the best suppliers, and a focus on supplier diversity is an important part of how we do that."

13

The State of Supplier Diversity Programs

According to CVM Solutions, the supplier diversity industry has come to a fork in the road. One path leads to a place where the supplier diversity concept is firmly entrenched in the public and private landscape, where most companies and government agencies strive to increase their diverse spend year over year. The other path leads to a place where companies do not take advantage of the growing potential of supplier diversity initiatives. Such companies will find themselves at a competitive disadvantage in the coming years.

CVM Solutions set out to discover what supplier diversity professionals are experiencing with their organizations' programs—the challenges they are facing, the ways that they manage and measure their programs, their thoughts about where supplier diversity is headed. CVM Solutions submitted a survey to supplier diversity professionals. These professionals have ringside seats to the trends that shape the industry and have a say in the policies and programs that will usher the industry into the future. More than 160 supplier diversity professionals and organizations, representing a variety of industries, took part in the study.

Their responses offer a telling story of the present and a compelling glimpse into the future of supplier diversity.

Survey Summary Findings

The comprehensive survey asked questions—some were multiple choice and some were open ended—about a variety of supplier diversity topics. Here are some of the highlights of the study:

© The Author(s) 2019
K. K. Porter, *Implementing Supplier Diversity*, https://doi.org/10.1007/978-3-319-94394-7_13

- 42% of respondents have supplier diversity programs that are at least ten years old.
- 72% of respondents cited corporate social responsibility as a top driver of supplier diversity.
- 53% of supplier diversity programs count small businesses in their diverse spend.
- 32% of respondents believe that their supplier diversity programs are very effective.
- 68% of respondents report that they track Tier II spend.
- 38% of respondents do not measure the financial return on investment (ROI) of their programs.
- 23% of respondents have a global supplier diversity program.
- 72% of respondents identify certification agencies as their primary means of finding diverse suppliers.

Below are some revealing graphics about the responses of the supplier diversity professionals surveyed through the study (Figs. 13.1, 13.2, 13.3, 13.4, 13.5, 13.6, 13.7, 13.8, 13.9, 13.10, 13.11, 13.12, 13.13, and 13.14).

What is your biggest challenge in the supplier diversity space?

- "Competing priorities. Lack of commitment at the upper-management level."
- "Changing the perception that diverse business equals less quality and more risks."
- "Convincing internal stakeholders to move away from 'brand-name' suppliers when able."

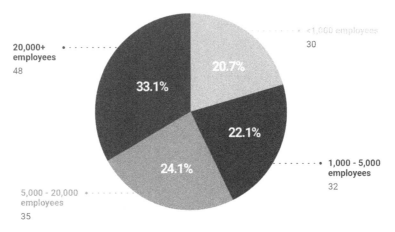

Fig. 13.1 How many employees work at your company? Source: CVM Solutions, State of Supplier Diversity Report—Supplier Diversity Programs (2017)

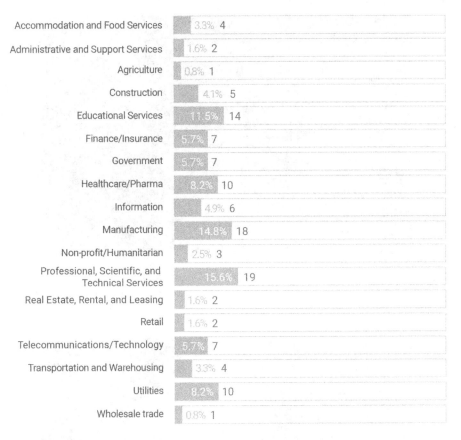

Fig. 13.2 Which industry/sector best corresponds to your organization. Source: CVM Solutions, State of Supplier Diversity Report—Supplier Diversity Programs (2017)

- "Developing a pool of MBE, WBE and DBEs to perform the work."
- "Ensuring MWOBs are consistently included in all competitive contracting opportunities."
- "Ensuring the supplier's diversity certification."
- "Finding and maintaining vendors that are diverse."
- "Finding diverse suppliers in the agencies category (creative agencies/digital agencies). Also, companies acquiring smaller, diverse companies greatly impact our diverse spend as we are technically not spending with a diverse supplier any more."
- "Finding diverse suppliers that can handle the requirements for our business."
- "Having more resources dedicated to supplier diversity."
- "Having the company realize it is a different sales vertical within the prospective supplier base."

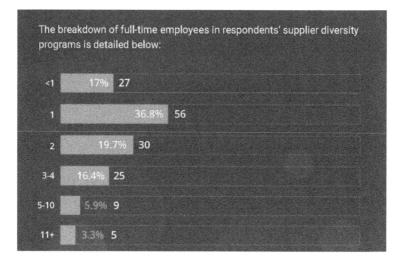

Fig. 13.3 How many full-time resources work for your supplier diversity program? Source: CVM Solutions, State of Supplier Diversity Report—Supplier Diversity Programs (2017)

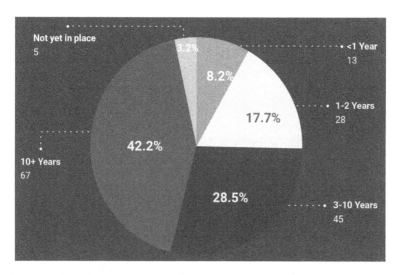

Fig. 13.4 How long has your supplier diversity program been in place? Source: CVM Solutions, State of Supplier Diversity Report—Supplier Diversity Programs (2017)

- "Having the right tools to measure and effectively communicating to all business units the importance of participating in finding diverse suppliers."
- "I wish we had more diverse suppliers submitting proposals."
- "Identification of certified diverse firms; convincing self-certified firms to get certified."

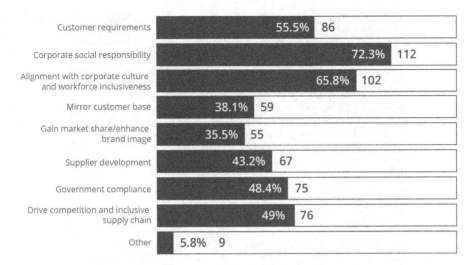

Fig. 13.5 What are the primary drivers of your supplier diversity program? Source: CVM Solutions, State of Supplier Diversity Report—Supplier Diversity Programs (2017)

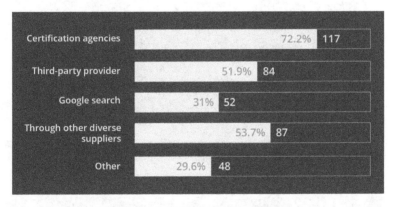

Fig. 13.6 How do you locate diverse suppliers? Source: CVM Solutions, State of Supplier Diversity Report—Supplier Diversity Programs (2017)

- "Identifying diverse suppliers that can scale and grow rapidly with us."
- "Identifying qualified suppliers in specialty spaces."
- "Large diverse vendors do a great job, but some of the small vendors need a lot of mentoring. Easily determining the economic impact."
- "My biggest challenge is wanting to spread the word about supplier diversity across the whole company and receiving a positive response. Getting all business units involved in supplier diversity."
- "State rules that require low bid, with very little wiggle room for diverse suppliers to compete."

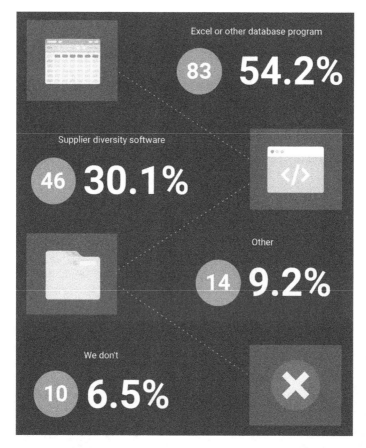

Fig. 13.7 How do you manage your diverse suppliers? Source: CVM Solutions, State of Supplier Diversity Report—Supplier Diversity Programs (2017)

Fig. 13.8 What percentage of your Tier I supplier spend is with diverse suppliers? Source: CVM Solutions, State of Supplier Diversity Report—Supplier Diversity Programs (2017)

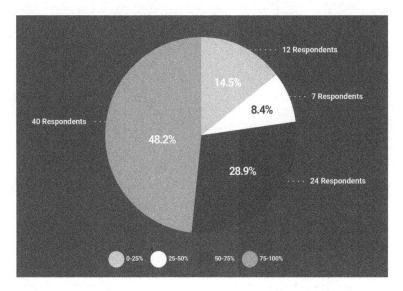

Fig. 13.9   What percentage of diverse suppliers who won a bid met or exceeded expectations of quality, efficiency, and cost savings last year? Source: CVM Solutions, State of Supplier Diversity Report—Supplier Diversity Programs (2017)

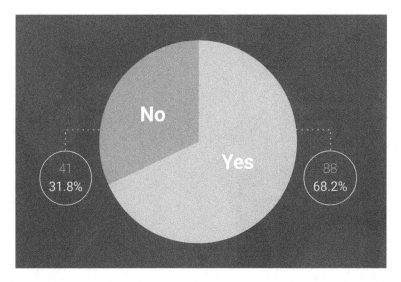

Fig. 13.10   Do you measure Tier II spend? Source: CVM Solutions, State of Supplier Diversity Report—Supplier Diversity Programs (2017)

- "The belief that supplier diversity is no longer necessary. Additionally, the old model for supplier diversity doesn't fit the new reality. If it's to meet the ever-more-diverse customer base, customers are not saying they care. In other words, customers, investors, shareholders, board members need more education to make bolder demands and to do so publicly."

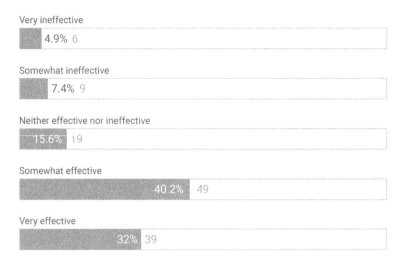

Fig. 13.11 How effective would you say your supplier diversity program is? Source: CVM Solutions, State of Supplier Diversity Report—Supplier Diversity Programs (2017)

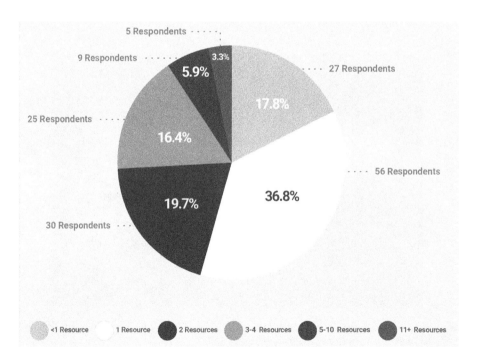

Fig. 13.12 How many full-time resources work for your supplier diversity program? Source: CVM Solutions, State of Supplier Diversity Report—Supplier Diversity Programs (2017)

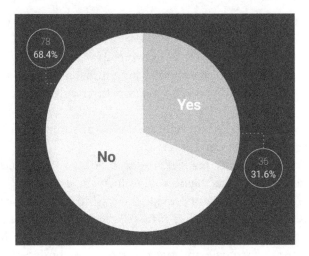

Fig. 13.13 Do you measure the economic impact of your program? Source: CVM Solutions, State of Supplier Diversity Report—Supplier Diversity Programs (2017)

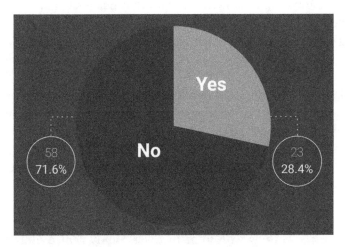

Fig. 13.14 Does your organization plan to implement a global supplier diversity program in the next three years? Source: CVM Solutions, State of Supplier Diversity Report—Supplier Diversity Programs (2017)

- "The biggest challenge in the supplier diversity space is diverse suppliers not taking the necessary steps to identify their weaknesses and then utilizing the right resources to close those gaps. If they want to compete with the bigger companies, they must be better and not rely on the diversity card. … The mentality of they can do everything (e.g., HR, accounting, procurement, IT and so on) great is a hindrance to their success. … One of the biggest weaknesses I see with a lot of diverse suppliers is their inability to manage their costs, which results in them trying to increase pricing to maintain their margins."

What do you enjoy most about supplier diversity?

- "Advocating for equity, diversity and inclusion and seeing the reality of real-time/real-life contracts for all. Making inroads for small business concerns beyond supplier diversity to a competitive culture of equality for all businesses."
- "Ability to see (while not currently measured) the impact our diverse suppliers have on the community."
- "As the supplier diversity manager, I get to go to a ton of really inspiring and cultured events. I like being able to help small or startup diverse suppliers get a foot in the door or provide them with advice to grow their business. The company I work for is Native American-owned and started in a garage, and now we are very successful, so it is always nice to be able to share our story of struggle and success with other businesses in the same shoes and offer advice and help with certifications and landing business. We believe it is imperative to give back."
- "Being a part of something meaningful that positively impacts our brand and sales."
- "Being able to support the community and grow the economy."
- "Being able to support the growth and inclusion of diverse companies in our communities."
- "Building the program and developing different approaches to sourcing strategies. Expanding the company's social responsibility platform."
- "Creating an inclusive supply chain and economic opportunities for historically underutilized suppliers."
- "Giving qualified diverse suppliers an opportunity to compete against larger companies."
- "Growing the economy; building relationships; saving money."
- "Helping to support a wide range of businesses."
- "I enjoy most working with so many diverse and talented individuals who can help bring unique perspectives and solutions to our needs."
- "I have been in supplier diversity for almost twelve years and love the opportunities it creates for diverse firms. Supplier diversity it not just a social service action; it creates communities of opportunity, creativity, and jobs—we are helping to build up our communities!"

14

Supplier Diversity Program Resources: For Practitioners and Entrepreneurs

As the supplier diversity industry has grown, so too have the availability and the depth of resources designed to help supplier diversity programs and entrepreneurs interested in interacting with them. The list below, though not exhaustive, is a great place to start:

Advocacy and Education

- Billion Dollar Roundtable (BDR)
- Business Matchmaking
- Institute for Supply Management (ISM)
- Small Business Administration (SBA)

  – 8(a) Business Development Program
  – HUBZone (Historically Underutilized Business Zones) Program

- The Latino Coalition
- National Veteran-Owned Business Association (NaVOBA)
- US Business Leadership Network
- National Association of Women Business Owners (NAWBO)
- WEConnect International
- Women Presidents' Organization (WPO)
- Minority Business Development Agency (MBDA)
- National Utilities Diversity Council (NUDC)
- Healthcare Supplier Diversity Alliance (HSDA)
- Airport Minority Advisory Council (AMAC)
- National Association of Educational Procurement (NAEP)

© The Author(s) 2019
K. K. Porter, *Implementing Supplier Diversity*, https://doi.org/10.1007/978-3-319-94394-7_14

Chambers of Commerce

- Asian/Pacific Islander American Chamber of Commerce and Entrepreneurship (ACE)
- National Black Chamber of Commerce (NBCC)
- National LGBT Chamber of Commerce (NGLCC)
- United States Hispanic Chamber of Commerce (USHCC)

Certifying Agencies

- National LGBT Chamber of Commerce (NGLCC)
- National Minority Supplier Development Council (NMSDC)
- National Veteran Business Development Council (NVBDC)
- Veterans Affairs (VA)

    - Vets First Verification Program

- Women's Business Enterprise National Council (WBENC)
- National Women Business Owners Corporation (NWBOC)
- US Business Leadership Network (USBLN)
- Disability Supplier Diversity Program (DSDP)

Research and Analytics Companies

- B2Gnow
- ConnXus
- CVM Solutions

Global (Affiliates through NMSDC)

- Australian Indigenous Minority Supplier Council (AIMSC)
- Canadian Aboriginal & Minority Supplier Council (CAMSC)
- Minority Supplier Development China (MSD-China)
- Minority Supplier Development UK (MSD-UK)
- South African Supplier Diversity Council (SASDC)

15

Conclusion: The "Next" Supplier Diversity Disruption: Supplier Inclusion

Supplier diversity has passed through several phases since its inception. It has moved from the "compliance" phase to the "right thing to do" phase to the "business case" phase. As business evolves and as demographics change, it is likely that there will be another seismic shift in the arguments for supplier diversity. It may be the case that the next disruption will take the arguments full circle, so that supporters of supplier diversity again tout the transformation of communities as the prime justification for supplier diversity. Communities are strengthened and renewed when successful, diverse entrepreneurs support employment, contribute to the tax base, and improve the economic health of communities by increasing income and consumption. Increasingly, corporate leaders want to know that their economic support is partly responsible for these transformations.

Economists talk of the circular flow of an economic system. One person's spend is another person's income, and the interactions between buyers and sellers have long-term, measurable effects. A $100 million project with a large city can lead to marked increases in minority employment in the city and new consumption by minority consumers. I believe that companies will want to understand this economic impact analysis as they decide with whom to spend their money.

When making predictions about the future of supplier diversity, it is crucial to examine the role that technology—particularly disruptive technology—is likely to play. Amazon is one of the best examples of such technological disruptions in the supply chain. Not only is the company challenging Walmart, but also it is pushing into the world of medical supply distribution and wholesaling. These changes affect consumers, hospitals, and even national and global supply chains. A company like Facebook, which boasts more than two

© The Author(s) 2019
K. K. Porter, *Implementing Supplier Diversity*, https://doi.org/10.1007/978-3-319-94394-7_15

billion members, has the potential to create their own sustainable economies, complete with their own currencies (e.g., Bitcoin).

It is not just diverse suppliers who will be impacted by these technologies. The organizations that support suppliers will also be hit hard by such disruptions. Information about companies is becoming cheaper and easier to collect. In the near future, databases of certified diverse suppliers will not be monopolized by diversity organizations like the National Minority Supplier Development Council (NMSDC) or the Women's Business Enterprise National Council (WBENC). If those organizations are no longer the sole sources of information about diverse suppliers, then their value to the market is likely to wane, which will spark strategic discussions within organizations about the appropriate level of engagement with those organizations.

If diverse businesses are concentrated in industries and with companies that will be the victims of technological disruption, there will be trouble ahead. In a more data-driven digital age, supplier diversity will have to change in order to survive. But it has evolved many times in the past, so there is no reason that it can't evolve again in the future.

In closing, I would like to share some optimistic words from the 2018 CVM Solutions "State of Supplier Diversity Report—Supplier Diversity Programs." When asked the question "Where do you see supplier diversity going in the next 3–5 years?" this is what some of them had to say:

- "Continued globalization of supplier diversity, and MWBEs having supplier diversity program initiatives."
- "As more suppliers are aware of their options, I believe there will be more certified diverse suppliers."
- "Continued growth and increase."
- "Global, I hope!"

If we make wise decisions about how to engage with businesses and how to use technology to our advantage, I believe that the optimists will be proven right.

References

Articles

Aarts, Deborah. "A League of Your Own," *Profit*, May 2011.

Flynn, Tom. "Improving Supplier Diversity Programs," *Lavante: A PRGX Company*, 17 May 2010, http://www.lavante.com/the-hub/supplier-information-management/improving-supplier-diversity-programs/.

Greene, M.V., et al. "Billion Dollar Roundtable: Supplier Diversity Best Practices," *MBN Custom Publications*, 2012.

The Hackett Group, "Supplier Diversity Does Not Drive Increased Costs," 27 Feb. 2008, http://www.thehackettgroup.com/about/alerts/alerts_2006/alert_08172006.jsp.

The Hackett Group. "Top Supplier Diversity Programs Broaden Value Proposition to Drive Increased Market Share, Other Revenue Opportunities," 16 Feb. 2017, https://www.thehackettgroup.com/news/top-supplier-diversity-programs-broaden-value-proposition/.

Hernandez, Richard J. "The Evolution of Supplier Diversity," Feb. 2004, http://www.e-mbe.net/tutorials/supplierdiversity/nc-the_evolution_of_supplier_diversity_feb2004.pdf.

National Women's Business Council. "Supply and Demand Perspectives on Women's Participation in Corporate Supplier Diversity Programs," 7 Dec. 2016, https://www.nwbc.gov/2016/12/07/research-on-supply-and-demand-perspectives-on-womens-participation-in-corporate-supplier-diversity-programs/.

Suarez, John. "11 Reasons to Invest in a Supplier Development Program," *CVM Solutions*, 1 Sept. 2017, https://blog.cvmsolutions.com/invest-in-a-supplier-development-program.

Supplier Lifecycle Management. "The Growing Business Imperative for Supplier Diversity," 2011, https://www.dnb.com/content/dam/english/dnb-solutions/supply-management/the_growing_business_imperative_for_supplier_diversity.pdf.

© The Author(s) 2019
K. K. Porter, *Implementing Supplier Diversity*, https://doi.org/10.1007/978-3-319-94394-7

Winkler, Jennifer. "The Small Business Administration's 8(a) Program: An Historical Perspective on Affirmative Action," *GW Policy Perspectives*, 1995.

Worthington, Ian. "Corporate Perceptions of the Business Case for Supplier Diversity: How Socially Responsible Purchasing Can 'Pay.'" *Journal of Business Ethics*, vol. 90, no. 1, Nov. 2009.

Sharma, Raj. "The Evolving Case for Supplier Diversity: 3 things you can do to make the most impact on your supplier diversity program." Supply & Demand Chain Executive, Nov. 2007. Accessed August 14, 2018, https://www.sdcexec.com/home/article/10289664/the-evolving-case-for-supplier-diversity.

McKinney, Jeffrey. "45 GREAT MOMENTS IN BLACK BUSINESS – No. 6: Maynard Jackson Becomes Atlanta's First Black Mayor." Black Enterprise Magazine, August 2018. Accessed 08/14/2018. http://www.blackenterprise.com/maynard-jackson-atlantas-first-black-mayor/.

Donelson, III Jimmy. "Closing Racial Wealth Gap: Power of Supplier Diversity." The Greenlining Institute, May 29, 2018. Accessed August 14, 2018, http://greenlining.org/press/2018/closing-racial-wealth-gap-power-of-supplier-diversity/.

Caron, Sarah. "14 Big Businesses That Started in a Recession." Inside CRM. Accessed August 16, 2018. http://www.insidecrm.com/articles/crm-blog/14-big-businesses-that-started-in-a-recession-53520/.

Samaniego, Adrianna; Gardner, Adam; Genteel, Chris; Greenhalgh, Leonard. Supply Chain 24. "Google's Pioneering Approach to Supplier Diversity." Accessed August 16, 2018. http://www.supplychain247.com/article/googles_pioneering_approach_to_supplier_diversity.

Tippens, Brian. Supplier Diversity: Economic Inclusion." Accessed August 16, 2018. https://www.diversitybestpractices.com/sites/diversitybestpractices.com/files/import/embedded/anchors/files/16_gdp_supplier_diversity.pdf.

Websites

Ewing Marion Kauffman Foundation
SBDC
Small Business Administration (SBA)
Billion Dollar Roundtable (BDR)
Business Matchmaking
Institute for Supply Management (ISM)
8(a) Business Development Program
HUBZone (Historically Underutilized Business Zones) Program
The Latino Coalition
National Veteran-Owned Business Association (NaVOBA)

US Business Leadership Network
National Association of Women Business Owners (NAWBO)
WEConnect International
Women Presidents' Organization (WPO)
Minority Business Development Agency (MBDA)
National Utilities Diversity Council (NUDC)
Healthcare Supplier Diversity Alliance (HSDA)
Airport Minority Advisory Council (AMAC)
National Association of Educational Procurement (NAEP)
Asian/Pacific Islander American Chamber of Commerce and Entrepreneurship (ACE)
National Black Chamber of Commerce (NBCC)
National LGBT Chamber of Commerce (NGLCC)
United States Hispanic Chamber of Commerce (USHCC)
National Minority Supplier Development Council (NMSDC)
National Veteran Business Development Council (NVBDC)
Veterans Affairs (VA)
Vets First Verification Program
Women's Business Enterprise National Council (WBENC)
National Women Business Owners Corporation (NWBOC)
Disability Supplier Diversity Program (DSDP)
B2Gnow
ConnXus
CVM Solutions
Australian Indigenous Minority Supplier Council (AIMSC)
Canadian Aboriginal & Minority Supplier Council (CAMSC)
Minority Supplier Development China (MSD-China)
Minority Supplier Development UK (MSD-UK)
South African Supplier Diversity Council (SASDC)

Books

Collins, Jim. *Good to Great*, Harper Business, 2001.
Peters, Tom, and Robert Waterman. *In Search of Excellence*, Jr. Harper Business, 1982 (first edition).
Porter, Kathey K. and Hoffman, Andrea. *50 Billion Dollar Boss: African American Women Sharing Stories of Success in Entrepreneurship and Leadership*, Palgrave Macmillan, 2015.
Hoskins, Michelle and Williams, Jean. *Sweet Expectations: Michelle Hoskins Recipe for Success*, Blue Ash, OH: Adams Media, 2004.

Reports

Billion Dollar Roundtable, "An Integrated Approach to Fostering the Use of Diverse Businesses," 2009.

The Hackett Group, "The Hackett Group Supplier Diversity Study," 2018.

National Minority Supplier Diversity Council, "Best Practices in Minority Supplier Development Guidelines," 2007.

National Minority Supplier Diversity Council, "Guidelines for Second Tier Initiative: Maximizing Opportunities for Minority-Owned Businesses," 2004.

Stawiski, Sarah, Ph.D., et al. "Employee Perceptions of Corporate Social Responsibility," 2010.

Beavers, Danielle, and Chen, Stephanie, "Supplier Diversity Report Card: California's Public Utilities," 2017.

Rawat, Naveen. "History of Purchasing," 10 July 2009, http://navpurchasing.blogspot.com/2009/07/history-ofpurchasing.html.

Index

CPSIA information can be obtained
at www.ICGtesting.com
Printed in the USA
LVHW091342020619
619879LV00009B/592/P